DIRTY LITTLE SECRETS

Nandita Chakraborty

Clever Fox
PUBLISHING

Chennai • Bangalore

CLEVER FOX PUBLISHING
Chennai, India

Published by CLEVER FOX PUBLISHING 2021

Copyright © Nandita Chakraborty 2021

All Rights Reserved.
ISBN: 978-93-93229-09-0

This book has been published with all reasonable efforts taken to make the material error-free after the consent of the author. No part of this book shall be used, reproduced in any manner whatsoever without written permission from the author, except in the case of brief quotations embodied in critical articles and reviews.

The Author of this book is solely responsible and liable for its content including but not limited to the views, representations, descriptions, statements, information, opinions and references ["Content"]. The Content of this book shall not constitute or be construed or deemed to reflect the opinion or expression of the Publisher or Editor. Neither the Publisher nor Editor endorse or approve the Content of this book or guarantee the reliability, accuracy or completeness of the Content published herein and do not make any representations or warranties of any kind, express or implied, including but not limited to the implied warranties of merchantability, fitness for a particular purpose. The Publisher and Editor shall not be liable whatsoever for any errors, omissions, whether such errors or omissions result from negligence, accident, or any other cause or claims for loss or damages of any kind, including without limitation, indirect or consequential loss or damage arising out of use, inability to use, or about the reliability, accuracy or sufficiency of the information contained in this book.

Literary Agent - First Forays Literary Agency
@Lalitha Ravindran

Book cover Illustrated by Rohit Bhasi

About:

A Bengaluru based illustrator, painter, mural artist and occasionally a graphic designer (now you know where digital lies in his scheme of things). He used to write a lot once, but oh well.

His body of work is a personal interpretation of the various myths, tales and belief systems that populate this part of the world where he is from. In other words, a humble endeavour to celebrate people and cultures, and their evolving relationships with the world around them.

The human body in all its beauty and imperfections, and the human mind with all its potential for creation, destruction and spinning stories, have always been his biggest muses. Guess that explains a leaning towards performing arts and artistes in general.

Website: https://indigoranges.in/pages/about-me
Facebook: https://www.facebook.com/Indigoranges/
Instagram: https://www.instagram.com/indigoranges/

Dedication

"To every Sumi, every Susan, every Evie, every Kim and within the mirror of every other women and men we live."

REVIEWS

Roanna Gonsalves

Author of The Permanent Resident, Winner of 2018 NSW Premier Literary multicultural awards.

This is a story of a brave woman coming to terms with her own fragility and failings as well as her boundless power. Across the physical spaces of India and Australia, sinking to the depths of sorrow, rising to moments of insight, this story is a no-holds-barred account of what it means to lose oneself, to find oneself again, and to hold space in desire, courage and strength.

Kishwar Chowdhury

2nd Runner up Masterchef Australia 2021.

The bravery it takes to sit down and confront yourself, inquire where the universe is leading you and take an altruistic look at your own life is truly difficult.

You have done this so wholeheartedly. It's a confronting task and I think you have undertaken it with honesty and real intention. I am enjoying traveling with you from Melbourne to various places and times through India.

What I love most is going on your journey of love. Whether that's with a partner, a friend, a parent or with your own self.

We all learn so much through the conversations, connections and stories we share with our friends. Reading this made me feel like I was sitting with you over a cup of chai, listening to you tell your life story so openly and wholeheartedly.

A book that will reach out to many who are weathering the highs and lows of "growing up" and just following their hearts along their journey.

I am so proud of you for writing this, Nandita.

Nishant Kaushik
Author of A Romance with Chaos, My Father Is a Hero, Chaos Project

Nandita Chakraborty's *Dirty Little Secrets* is a riveting, breezy read. Separating the tone from the theme of the story is a difficult art, but the author demonstrates this skill with flair.

Dirty Little Secrets is a no-holds barred account of a young woman's travails with life, and her adventures and misadventures en route to discovering and embracing her identity. Even as the protagonist takes you along a journey peppered with hope and angst alike, the tongue-in-cheek humour ensures a smile as you flip each page.

Make this an essential read for the season.

Niharika Puri
Author and Screenwriter

Nandita Chakraborty narrates her life with typical candour, sincerity, vulnerability and a rare self-awareness that is refreshing to behold. Her story will have you engrossed, taking you from her tidy, Australian life to the vibrant chaos of her hometown and family in India. The sights and sounds are as palpable as the wonderfully-etched characters she meets. You're in for a ride!

Simran Gulati

Mrs India Global 2018, Actor and Entrepreneur

I am not sure if I have the words to describe what I have read so far. I was hooked by the third paragraph of the 'Prologue' and the end has left me longing for more. Your quest, questions and discovery of love is very relatable to the audience as we have all been there at some point in time. The circumstances may be different but the feeling and emotions you went through is something we all have had. I really enjoyed reading about your personal challenges and how you coped with them. Your fresh outlook when you met someone that took me back to having butterflies when I was at that stage in my life.

I loved how you wrote the book so far and your spiritual beliefs and your explanations of Indian culture, God and food. So far, my all-time favourite part is the excerpt of Shiv Ling.

Nandita! You are a born writer and I love your talent of grasping your audience with your words and longing for more. I can't wait to keep reading.

Binnu Singh

Jewels by Binnu Singh; Diamond Designer – New Delhi

I found it to be a journey of a woman from India (a conservative society) to an open society of Australia. The transformation from a girl to a woman. The heartache, the pain, love and wisdom.

The story touches deeply and I think any woman can resonate with it. *It's a must Read.*

Beau Hillier

Award winning writer of short stories and editor.

Dirty Little Secrets opens with a quote by Tagore on optimism and perseverance, and the book *Dirty Little Secrets* is a celebration of a singular journey to find that optimism.

Nandita Chakraborty is raw and honest in her self-examination, sharing herself with readers as she flees Australia to escape a mortifying incident, finds herself lost in India as she tries to reconnect with her original homeland, and faces an uncertain but liberated future after a life-defining accident.

A memoir of life and longing in Australia and India, the book is an evocative meditation on love, life, family and belonging.

CONTENTS

Reviews v
Prologue xi
Author's Note xvii
Introduction xix

SCANDALS OF MELBOURNE – 2010 1
ISABELLE 9
VAMP SLAYER 33
THE POLICE FILES 49
THERAPY FOR LIFE 54
THE MOVE 61
AUGUST 2011 64
NEW DELHI – JANUARY 2011 76
BABLI 84
THE FESTIVAL OF COLOUR 96
THE MISSING PEACE 126
DIARIES OF ME 164
CHOICES – JUNE 2011 179
THE ACCIDENT – NOVEMBER 2011 202
23 DECEMBER 2011 234
9 SEPTEMBER 2016 242

Epilogue 248
Acknowledgements 251
About the Author 254

PROLOGUE

As I sit to write this prologue, I reminisce about the year behind me, which is a blur not only to me, but also to many others. The year 2020 has been a year of reflection. Most of us dwindled somewhat, lapsing momentarily in the hands of time. I was no different, while trying to reflect on the past decade that was gone in a wink of an eye.

So, I ponder my memoir and events that took place ten years ago, changing my life forever in 2010. If I hadn't gone through all that I have transcribed in these pages, then I wouldn't be the woman I am today. I have described myself as a cat having nine lives. Why? In Ram Gopal Verma's *Bhoot*, a cat dies in the middle of the film and by the last scene it's back again. Any cynical person would be saying that it's just a bluff; some would say that it has always been there, just not visible.

That's how I felt about myself: dead to the world and then suddenly back to life again. As the world is living through a pandemic now, I am sure this thought sits with most of us.

In this book, you will read about the people I have met, friendships, betrayals, love found and lost, society writing me off, and the universe giving me a chance to rediscover myself. A new birth. I have lived and seen the lives of others through their eyes. Sometimes I have lost track of time. Sometimes I wondered if I am in a short dream, or a shortened life in a never-ending dream. I have seen people walk in and out of my life, making space for new faces. Some chose to stay and others just left. It can be cruel, empty and hollow, undoing all that has been good.

In the last ten years, how many times have I said the words "I love you"? How many times have those words been reciprocated to me? Countless! And this happened regardless of the depth of context of the friendship. The only thing that has not changed is the act of betrayal, though that has transformed in its boundaries too. Generations come and go and things transform – and change is the only truth. So, when I penned my life in a diary, I wanted to change too. With that I thought society had changed as well, but the only thing that has changed is me; everything around me is still the same. Is this a good thing or a bad thing? I cannot make everyone happy; even if I try, I'll be falling short. I have decided in the last ten years that it's better to be loved by all than adored by one.

Ten years on, when I started writing this memoir, it was strictly for myself; many of my closest friends thought that I wouldn't have the nerve to share the most intimate details of my life. What's done is done; ridiculed or not, I needed to tell my story, as a souvenir for many women who are looking for an answer to the risk of relationships. I still may not be able to provide an answer, but maybe a slice of hope instead – it's okay to dive into a relationship. Even if I break down, I'll be okay.

It's a validation to myself that I am paying it forward to many who, like me, want help but are shy of speaking out. It is never too late – everyone has the luxury of time in which to free themselves. I know everyone tries to find a good scandal in any story; even if you haven't put your own story forward, people have already subscribed to the idea of writing you off. Each time you cross paths, you are judged. Do you have to pay the price every time? Are we willing to go through everything and throw away everything for a mere feeling?

When you open this book, just a caution: you will be plunged into the first chapters of a scandal. If you think it is your moral obligation to quote me with colourful adjectives like "childish", "insecure" or "what was she thinking", let me tell you – I have heard it all and nothing surprises me. I didn't make any public outrage; I quietly surrendered myself to time. I went through all these emotions and let me tell you, they were not good. I got confused; it was as if I was mourning for *me*.

When the blackmail took place in 2010, I left everything to go back to India, leaving behind friends and a life. I was prepared to travel back to the past. Did the temple bells and food help shape who I am today? I was there with the gods and goddesses, trying to understand the manifestation of life. Food played an important part then (and in my present too). I overindulged during my depression, yet it has never satisfied me more than writing about food in my present. But, here I was at the temples, wishing for the gods to exalt me from the pain – but secretly, I was wishing for love. That's how we are. I got love in return, tenfold – but not the love of a man. Yes, somewhere in between the divorce, cheating, scandals and infatuation, I managed to grasp love and then lose it to go on my own journey.

Dirty Little Secrets is also about the most intimate secrets I had with myself. Things that you wouldn't want your best friends to go through. I forgot to take care of me. Changing cities and people is not a solution – it is temporary.

During recovery from my accident in 2011, I was beginning to understand my dysfunctionality with love, my family and myself. I was vulnerable again, very close to making unreasonable decisions for myself. For the first time in a decade, I was now making decisions with my heart. I had no choice. The accident took away all the pain, the trepidation, the tribulations – there was this amazing peace around me. I was finally not in charge. Most of the time I didn't understand what my head was on about, as it was new territory – but in reality, it felt good not to be making decisions. Is a broken brain more effective than a broken heart? I think it is; my beautiful broken brain was a gift to me. I understood it perfectly well. It didn't matter anymore who was ruling what.

It did allow me to cry and grieve when my dad passed away in 2016; I was given an incentive to feel those emotions again, with a price of drifting away from my family. In 2017 it let me complete my novellas and took me to Paris. I was just beginning to feel that I could be in control again – but then, before I knew it I was troubled again. But this time it was a different type of love. Family love.

I was very close to losing my mother to her heart attacks. It was as if she lost the urge to live after Dad passed away and no one understood her grief. I did understand her, but pretended I didn't. She lost a partner of forty-eight years. I would grieve and create a fuss over losing someone I had just known for five years or six months. It hit me just then that grief is not selfish – but to love and not share the love is selfish. I may have inherited the strength from her but definitely did not inherit the love.

I promised myself that I would never fall in love again – and just like that, I felt an urge to fall in love again. It was a fateful meeting with Franklin just before the accident in 2011. As described in this book, he was sent to me to celebrate what love is and should be all about. I was not unhinged this time, because what I felt was real. Welcoming love came with forgiveness – not just to myself, but also to people I loved, including a few family members. I realised that no matter how dysfunctional a family is, love is forever there. Some choose to get clarity later in life and some choose not to, thinking it's too late. *It's never too late.*

The commentary can go on, but I think Franklin was a big lesson for me for all my past and future relationships.

I did make mistakes and forgot about myself several times because I was not willing to let go of the love I felt with Franklin. In 2016 my world came crashing down with losing my father, my dignity, my home and my cognition. Losing my heart to a younger man and being humiliated by him gave me the strength for this story to be told.

I cannot be selfish because love is not – I have made a few sincere mistakes, but it is all to create that space to adapt. I am not saying I wouldn't make any mistakes again and open my heart, but I can confirm one thing that I have learned over the last ten years: I will not let myself be bullied by conditional friendships, or by those who cannot fall in love or tell me otherwise. I will let myself be available for change and adapt to it. I have promised myself that – and it is important to convey my sincerity to hope, change and love.

Disclaimer: Read without prejudice – and if you want to judge, then do so by your perspective, not mine.

AUTHOR'S NOTE

All the events described in this book are real and factual. All the characters in this book are real. In most places, I've used real names; however, I've changed some names to respect privacy.

Without the people I've met in my life, I wouldn't have written a book today. I hope I've done justice to everyone, as they have influenced my life so much.

INTRODUCTION

> "I have become my own version of an optimist, if I can't make it through another door I'll go through another door – or I'll make a door. Something terrific will come no matter how dark the present."
>
> **Tagore**

I'm not a philosopher or a psychologist; I'm a normal human seeking my own motivation and my own experiences. I breathe and feel the same emotions we all do.

What is love? What does it mean to us? Have we grasped it yet, or do we just hold on to the idea to satisfy our loneliness? If anyone says they've found the love of their life, the perfect love, then good luck to them. They all might be delusional. After all, love can be an illusion.

I'm no expert, but I still cannot relate to the morbid idea that when things go pear-shaped, people decide to be just friends or run to the court to remove themselves from each other, when once their life together was a beautiful portrait.

To me there's always this equation, that one candidate has a strong chemistry – while the other is just there to be strung along by that chemistry.

However, I can contradict myself here, such as with the everlasting love of Romeo and Juliet: did Shakespeare go wrong with this myth, or was it his romanticism that has appealed to generations after generations to fall in love?

However, there are people who believe in arranged marriages, an alternate and quick way to find love. I've never understood this concept but I'm willing to grasp it, as there are fine examples in front of me. My parents were married for about forty-two years. But my mother was only sixteen when she got married; how would she have known what love was? Has she discovered it yet?

I cannot argue with her on this, as that's her own personal perspective. I tried to ask her if it was love and she would repeatedly tell me in her simple way, 'Forty-two years of marital bliss.' I dare not confront her anymore.

I could've asked the same of my father, but in this middle-class life of Indian people it would be rude, so I kept it to myself. Though, I would often hear him say when he was happy over a glass of whisky and ice, 'My partner of life, a partner who is there, strength to strength, in good and bad.' I still didn't get the word 'love' here but I could sense a feeling of security and longing.

In 65–70% of the Indian population, people get married for procreation. Later, it's the struggle for life.

Please don't misunderstand me – I'm not doing a critical census of India, I'm not laughing at my culture, and I'm not trying to divert my readers to a political debate of marriage and divorce.

All I want to know is, when does someone yearn for love? As children, we yearn for love from a tender age; it's received from our mothers, fathers, sisters and brothers. That's family bonding. Then in our adolescence, we yearn for a different love that can only be shared by two people. Is that love or is it just an attachment? That is what I'm trying to discover, and with that my own identity.

When I came to Australia, I came with this view, re-living someone else's dreams and growing up with certain values: study, get a job, get married at twenty. But I was at my 'use-by date' when I came to Melbourne. Here, I rediscovered myself in various forms. I thank this beautiful country and its people for accepting me for what I am. Here I tamed my wild heart, broke my heart and learned to mend it in different variations. I found myself here – only to be lost again.

This is when I decided I had to fly back to my roots, to return to the connection that I lost over the years. I believed that if I saw the glass as half-empty, I would lose it all. But I lost it all anyway, including the ability to trust and to love.

My connection with God over the years has lost its finesse. Was I responsible for this spiritual break-up? Or have I used a short-term excuse to run away from every piece of what I loved? Was I responsible for this or just overreacting?

With faint trepidation in my heart, I became determined to look at the situation differently. My glass is not completely empty, it's just half-filled. I still have my roots to fall back to: the warmth of my mother's hug, the wisdom of my father and my home to strengthen the soul.

Was this self-defense or running away from situations that I no longer wanted to confront? That was still to be discovered.

As a reader and a writer, I've tried to comprehend this verse and found it to be as my own interpretation of my life, as if I'm asking God to give me a new birth.

I'm not writing history, but I hope through these pages I re-introduce myself once again.

SCANDALS OF MELBOURNE – 2010

> "You have to keep breaking your heart until it opens."
>
> —Rumi

'Zoya, here is my resignation letter.'

Zoya looked at me. 'Are you sure? What happened?' I could see she was trying her best not to sound too shocked.

Still trying to remain calm, I smiled at her, feeling like a huge pressure valve was about to burst in my head. 'Actually, I really don't know where to begin. You know how before you left for your holidays, I told you about someone I met online from America? Well! He turned out to be a scammer!' I lowered my voice. 'He was trying to blackmail me.'

I realised that I had to be careful of what I said here. 'As crazy as this will sound, we actually intended to get married. Well, at least that was my intention.' I laughed sarcastically. 'I was actually getting married to a scammer. Well! As you can understand, people do adversely silly things when they're in a long-distance relationship … and, thinking that I was in one, I did something very stupid. As a result, I'm being blackmailed.'

There it was! I said it. I was embarrassed and hung my head in shame.

Zoya gave me a bewildered look and much to my surprise, I saw her eyes building up with tears – or it could have been a trick of her tired eyes fixing on me, without blinking. Raising her arms across my shoulders, she said, 'There is nothing to be embarrassed about. My cousin was in a similar situation – these things happen.'

We were interrupted by a knock at the door and asked to empty the room, as another business unit had previously booked the room for a meeting. I saw myself like a Bollywood heroine trapped in the ravines of Chambal, like the climax in *Sholay* (Bollywood's blockbuster of the 70s), where Veeru (the hero) comes to rescue Basanti (the heroine) from Gabbar (the villain).

I heard someone call my name; I thought it was Veeru from *Sholay* calling me, but to my relief it was Zoya. I scratched my head. Was I going mad?

I felt so embarrassed, not because I was discussing this with a senior colleague but because it was happening to me at thirty-five. I felt as if I had done something wrong, not only today but for the past few days, and everything happening around me was beyond my control. I felt guilty but I could not figure out what the guilt was about. It was a strange feeling.

My head held low and my heart racing, I sat down. 'I've been asked by the detective to cut all communications on social networking sites – in a way, hide my identity – and to cut all communications with *him*. I had to change my phone numbers, my email, I …' My voice grew louder in anger. When I spoke again I was polite. 'Unfortunately, my laptop blew up. It's gone for repairs so it's become inconvenient for the cops to track his IP address. They're still trying. I'm absolutely shocked; I never imagined it could be happening to me. I've seen movies and heard about these things but when I'm actually living every moment of it, it's surreal. He not only played with my emotions but also my family. He spoke to Sumita, my sister, to fix a marriage date!'

I smiled at Zoya, looking straight into her eyes. 'I need to get away from this situation for a while. I'm not running away ... all I need is to breathe again and assess where I went wrong. It may be the wrong decision but I don't want to regret any more in life – I have to get away to come back again. It's suffocating me.'

Zoya dropped her shoulders. 'Nandita, before I accept this resignation, I just wanted to ask you: have you discussed this with anyone apart from your sister? I want you to speak to a counsellor – our company provides this to all our employees for free. It's important that you take someone else's opinion; it will be confidential and it will help you. Maybe you should opt for a career break rather than resigning.'

Tears gathered in my eyes; my throat was almost choked. 'I've just spoken to Sumita, but I've already made up my mind, Zoya. I need to go back to my roots, to get in touch with myself. I want to take control before I lose control over myself. I want to break my routine, re-think where I belong ... perhaps write a book. I don't know what I want to do yet, but I need to go so that I'm able to think again.'

Realising that I was pleading my own resignation, Zoya said, 'You are a strong character – my hat's off to you. You carry your heart on your shoulders.'

I looked at her, running my fingers through my fringe, and I chuckled to lighten the mood. 'I think this is my mid-life crisis. I often wondered when people would say that in their sixties, but a mid-life crisis doesn't come knocking at your door, it just comes – so what if I'm thirty-five?'

Zoya laughed at this, which made me feel a little lighter too. Giving me a sympathetic look, she nodded in approval and said, 'If that's what you want then it's fine, but I would like you to speak to the counsellor. I will email you all the details. I totally agree with you, life is what you make of it – but love yourself and don't be so hard on yourself.'

I walked out of the office with a huge sigh of relief, as if an enormous weight had been lifted from my shoulders. I didn't know at the time why I felt so relaxed; was it because I didn't have to go through the routine of work? A natural therapy for the shattered spirit, I guess. On the contrary, I began to wonder: was this the right decision?

I suddenly became quite insecure. No job, no money – how would I cope without money and friends?

***

The next morning, I woke up with a slight headache. I looked at my watch and sprung straight up – it was 1.30 in the afternoon; thank God it was the weekend. The bottle of wine from last night hit me as the headache turned out to be a massive hangover.

I didn't want to go to the gym today.

My brain was racing and I felt hot; I was suffocating myself again with all kinds of unpleasant thoughts. I lit up a cigarette and scolded myself, *have to let go of this dirty habit,* but to be honest it really felt good. I got up from my bed and opened the blinds and window; it was beautiful outside and I felt alive again as the gush of fresh spring air touched my face. I decided it had to be a good day for a walk and I was racing towards the bathroom when a sharp pain churned inside my stomach. I knew I hadn't eaten anything from last night, and all I drank was wine.

My friend Isabelle's words rang in my ears: 'Wine is a stimulant to all stupidity, and it's not a solution.' Hmm …

Isabelle is always right! She always helped me out through her wisdom and I wished I listened to her more diligently.

I quickly had a shower, got changed and went to the pantry to see if there was anything to eat, as the fridge had been dead for over fifteen days now. I had no strength to think about what was happening around me. Was I being a victim or just acting like one?

Visions of Basanti came back to my mind, where she started dancing to the song 'Jab taak hain jaan maine nachunge' ('I shall dance until I have life'). I couldn't remember the rest of the song, as until now I never visualised a Bollywood film – even *Sholay*, of which I had only seen bits and pieces.

Like billions of people across the universe, I also dream; I would often fantasise myself as a character of any outlandish form: as a traveller in Paris who falls in love with a painter near the Eiffel Tower. Sometimes, in a beautiful red gown, I'm giving an acceptance speech for winning an award – or I'm a famous dancer with people showering me with accolades.

Then suddenly, one by one they all would vanish, forcing me back into reality: the taxis, the screeching brakes of the tram hitting the tracks, the sound of a harmonica played by a homeless man who awaits some generous donations from the city slickers passing by, and the bustling cafés with the 'ssheeshee' noise from their espresso machines.

However, having Basanti in my dreams was like icing on the cake; Basanti got my own dreams drifting. I sometimes thought people who dreamt like me didn't get what they wanted in life – this is the reason they get themselves wrapped up in their own superficial world. It's like comfort eating, but with dreaming for me.

However, everything happening in the present was not a bad dream. I pinched myself, squeezed my eyes and was still wide awake. I was indeed in the grip of reality.

Maybe it was a sign of India calling me? Was I really dancing to the tune of life? Perhaps my own dreams had become my own versions of love gone all wrong, or perhaps just a nightmare. I needed a reality check. With this confusion I realised one thing: that this relationship proved to be a real spoof, the most expensive price I ever paid in the name of love.

I stood in front of South Yarra Station with a coffee and looked around. Where did I want to go? Amid the rush of weekend trading, I felt like being happy, spending a lot of money and losing myself in the crowd. It was different today: I didn't want to be seen or heard. I grabbed my iPhone, turned it off and screamed, 'Taxi, to Brighton Beach please.'

When I reached the beach, it was around four in the afternoon and the sun was at its peak; it had been a glorious day so far. All I could hear was the sound of the waves hitting the rocks. There was no one around – just me, the sky, the ocean and my silence. Across the shore I could see the entire skyline of Melbourne. Its massive buildings reminded me of its hallowed ground. Like tin soldiers, we march our way to these concrete offices, devoid of emotions, suppressing them, believing that we would lose the cold walls that we've created to protect us.

As far as I could see, there was water and only water, calling me to swim across the other side. I took two steps forward to embrace the massive high tide wave that was quickly approaching me; I wanted to be engulfed. For a split second I couldn't breathe; I ran back, absolutely drenched, realising I was a coward.

I looked at the skyline again and this time I screamed with all my frustrations, crying out so loudly that all I could hear was my loud sobs. I kept on mumbling, 'Why me?' I wiped those tears and I began consoling myself with a hug. 'It's going to be okay … it's going to be okay.'

I knew my strength, but my soul was shattered; it felt difficult to replace it with new strength and endurance. Fatigue was slowly taking over my entire body; I sat on the sand hugging my knees and felt the hot sun right on top of me. I got lost again in my own thoughts; was I so selfish or naïve that I didn't realise what I was getting myself into? Did I always get hurt in my relationships because of my middle-class values of getting married? Perhaps sometimes the entire problem in a relationship is people setting marriage as a goal.

Who was I fooling? This new man was neither there to get married to me nor interested in a relationship. Sam was a fake, a cheater, a schemer who raped me of my emotions. Why did I let this happen to me again? I clasped my hands in anger at this thought. At that time, I didn't grasp Amit's intentions – nor could I comprehend now how many victims like me are out there, delirious with shock, contemplating whether to be loved or not to be loved again.

Was I too callous or insecure to look away from the dangers of Amit's schemes, or perhaps I let him take control of my emotions with his 'unending love' for me? I was foolish, and didn't learn my lesson, making the same foolish mistake from that same internet site. When I parted ways with Amit he not only loved himself, me and other women. Sadly, that ended in court, as I had to keep that psychotic man away from me. Is it my luck with men? So fragile!

Before Amit, there was Frank – that ended in court too. It was not that painful; I was hurt and distraught but maybe I wasn't looking at the bigger picture. Frank was no man from the internet; I was with him for five years until the sinking feeling of being a victim emerged again.

Siddhant was a colleague who used to work with me. He didn't want a relationship – all he wanted was to sleep with me. At least he was honest.

The only difference in this current situation was that this schemer was in America and we'd only chatted online and on the phone. We'd never met, we just exchanged photos and 'saw' each other online – and he was 'in love' with me. At the end, it was I who was paying for it.

I'd been thinking about getting in touch with my roots. I didn't know whether it was the right decision to go back to India – whether I would be able to re-introduce myself to the daring twenty-five year old Nandita I left behind in Delhi, ten years ago. A lot of history had happened between Delhi and me! I was uncertain again. But just then, I remembered our Guru Devraha jee's words: he always said, 'Age is history and each one of us is made up of our own history.' I smiled; maybe I could rewrite my history once again.

There was absolute silence around me – no more Bollywood films or rock bands haunting me. I felt a lot calmer and realised that it must have been hours since I'd come here. The fresh northerly winds were very welcoming; once again, nature with its amazing powers rejuvenated this broken soul.

As I rose up, I felt a sharp pain in my abdomen and my head felt dizzy; I soon realised it was not the sun, but I was still intoxicated from the bottle of wine last night.

I sat again for a while only to recall Isabelle's words. 'Alcohol is not a cure. It's a stimulant to all stupidity, it's not a solution.' I broke into a smile.

 # ISABELLE

> "If you tell the truth, you don't have to remember anything."
>
> —Mark Twain

Isabelle was the woman who discovered that I had turned myself knowingly in to the hands of a schemer.

She was forty-three years old and slender, with a slight dimple on her left cheek (which remains almost unnoticed) and a blond fringe resting on her forehead. Her light brown eyes were protected with glasses that camouflaged her crow's feet. Tight, fitted, designer-style dresses draped dangerously on her beautiful slim body.

I gave her one hundred percent; most people her age could be either struggling at the gym to get a body like hers or simply be lost in the hustle and bustle of life. What was her secret? No gym, just a healthy diet minus sugar (with the occasional binge). Her cooking skills would always put me to shame; her excellent communication skills and her intelligence are god-gifted.

To most of us who knew Isabelle, she was an extrovert, because she often spoke her mind – and when she broke into a deep laughter, you could almost swear that you're listening to a bubbly sixteen year old at a high school prom – but in reality, she could be extremely shy.

I always felt at home with her whenever we would chat, sometimes for hours over the phone. I used to think I was the talkative one, but after meeting Isabelle I had finally met my match.

I met Isabelle when I was seconded to another department in the company in September 2008. She would always pass with a smile whenever we crossed each other's desks. We would often exchange greetings in the morning, as we felt quite timid and awkward; not only was it a new department, but we were new to each other.

One day as I was crossing her desk, I overheard her speaking to another colleague about love and relationships. At that time, I didn't understand her, as I felt intimidated by the women in that department.

Sometimes the women would talk about their ignorant perception of India. I didn't blame them, nor did I do anything to change their views – in fact, I supported their ignorance. I travelled both lands, walked both their streets, wore both their shoes. But somewhere in between, it threw me in pandemonium. Something had changed in my life; I didn't know what it was. I had yet to discover it.

We would often exchange our views on relationships. She was going through her own turmoil with her ex and I was on a yo-yo with my then lover, who was busy chasing other lovelies. Issy was then looking after her late mother and would often vent her frustrations with us about her.

All these little conversations were during coffee breaks and her cigarette break; I would just find an excuse to go down to smell nicotine, as quitting cold turkey was difficult. The things we do for the men in our lives! She would join me for my kati roll sessions and I'd watch her ridiculous sweat moustache as she said, 'It's not chilli hot, it's fire hot!' On one hand, she would be rubbing her forehead with a tissue, but on the other hand she was enjoying it plentifully.

We were just two ordinary women who discovered an amazing strength in each other's company. Issy would always say that I helped her during her difficult times with her ex by mentally supporting her, but I always felt it was the other way around.

Someone told me a while back that in life, we humans cross paths to deliver someone from their crisis or redeem them. To be honest, we both didn't know how and when we were seeking redemption, and in what form we'd touched each other's lives. It was special!

Her two gorgeous girls, Bessie and Jenny, were her pride and joy. Often when I called her, I would hear her scream, 'Jenny, stop it!' Jenny, being the boisterous kelpie, would always dominate Issy and Bessie with her half-human attitude. The barking wouldn't stop though, and the screams would become louder, with Bessie and Jenny barking back at her in unison.

Issy would always put her two girls before anything. As an organised person, she would take time to see the vet, shop for their food and look for the best accommodation to spoil her two lovely bitches.

It was during the Christmas of 2008 that Issy and I could say that we really became close. We chose to spend Christmas together at my place, as she didn't want to go to her brother's and I didn't want to be with my sis and her family for a picnic. I was hurting and wanted to be alone, because Amit left for India on a holiday, leaving me with a countdown until his return – only to discover he was returning with someone else in his heart.

So, we girls decided to have a blast together. I treated her to some fantastic tandoori chicken and my infamous kati rolls, and she made some amazing Christmas pudding, which left me licking my lips for days. After lots of coffees, we realised that we were similar in many ways and were honoured to be happy in each other's company. We choked ourselves smoking menthol cigarettes (I decided that day I'd rather be a chimney), and cracked ourselves gasbagging about the different sizes and shades of men we came across in our lives. We swapped sex stories, asking ourselves: what makes men tick? Or, to be clearer, what was their perception on satisfying women?

We would gasp at each other's stories and she would sometimes sigh at how my lover boy was so unsatisfactory when it came to my needs. I found out that day that men can be replaced!

It made sense; after all, I was not with a man, but a 'horny' toy, who was always on the prowl for his next victim. I learned a few tricks of my own too; I learned to fake every orgasm while with him. He might be feeling great about his manhood but I always had the last laugh. A lesson to learn here: no compromise when it comes to a woman's need!

Over the years, we drifted apart a bit; the daily conversations ended up as weekly chitchats, then it turned into per calendar month. I guess we had caught the virus called 'life'. While she found love, I was still at a fragile stage with all the colourful men who had been walking in and out of my life – it was taking an immense toll on me, leaving me absolutely drained.

At one point during our friendship I may have offended Issy, a serious and unintended mistake on my part. I had come to know a mutual friend whom I was dating for a short while. One evening I hung up on Issy to take his call; she reckoned I had done this frequently in the past. Maybe my quest for love and my fixation on the male kingdom was overwhelming, though that makes me sound like a man-eater – in reality I was just like any other ordinary woman, seeking just one man and one love.

I always felt a sense of protection around Issy, especially when it came to men. I remember when I was with this 'mutual friend' and he'd invited me to his place on our first date. She demanded an answer: 'Why did you go to his place?' Her yell, by the way, still sends a nervous message to the brain: 'Run baby run, it's Issy calling!'

When I look back today at our friendship, I comprehend that the space she needed was not out of sheer avoidance, but for me to rediscover myself. In other words, she wanted me to grow up – or perhaps she wanted me to experience my own journey, my way. Sometimes, silence speaks a thousand words and sometimes that's what true friends do: set up the foundation of realisation.

***

'Congratulations! Ninty, I'm very happy for you.' Issy sounded very excited. She'd always call me by this nickname; I have several names but this one is unique.

Nandita is quite a difficult name to pronounce in the West. In India, it would often be pronounced as Non-dita or Nun-deeta. To be honest, I love all the beautiful nouns that I've scored over the years in Melbourne: Naan, Nani, Nandos, Nintendo, Chucky and Ninty. My favourite was all of them, except Naan! I would cringe! It made me 'edible' and reminded me of Indian naan bread.

A bewildered tone in Issy's voice made me a little uneasy and I felt I needed to protect myself here. But it was Issy, after all – why was I being hesitant? Was it the fact that I didn't want to share this little secret of mine, so no one could influence me? Sheer nervousness was already forming in the back of my mind. The love and romance that was bestowed upon me over the past few weeks was surreal and I didn't want anyone to be envious about it. But, it was Issy – I was always comfortable with her. We spoke about everything and this romance of the past few weeks shouldn't be more important than a friendship of a lifetime.

'Guess what? I also found a Mr Scottish like you,' I said.

I could hear Issy laughing and that put me at ease. Earlier that day I had emailed her a photo of Sam.

'He looks good and you both make a cute couple,' she said. 'I was always sure after the debacle with Amit ... actually, pretty sure that you wouldn't go for an Indian or Asian this time.'

I had emailed the wedding card to Issy that Sam had designed for our wedding, which had my photo and his on the background, and the most beautiful poetry dedicated to me: 'My love will last forever.' It was too good to be true indeed.

'Well! It's not my scene at all, all those mushy, lovey dovey romantic words, but it's so much you – you believe in fairy tales and I can see you with that. Oh, well! Again, everyone is different and I'm so very happy.'

I wished Issy could see how happy I was right now. 'Issy, he is forty and I really do believe that this time it's for real. Sometimes things just happen – you know I believe in love at first sight. I've finally hit the jackpot, love, it's finally happening; I'm getting married, yippee!'

Issy said, 'I know you're very happy, but again, how did you manage to decide to get married so soon? You haven't met each other and it's so important that you guys first meet. What did your sis have to say to all this?' She sounded very skeptical now; I knew Issy always had my best interests in mind, and she was concerned about me.

'Relax, Issy! This time I made sure it's all okay – it takes a lot for a man in his forties to commit to marriage. Actually, he was trying his luck on Indian sites, as he's very inspired by Indian culture; he has an Indian friend and sees how well he is treated by his wife. He's suffered a lot of hurt and deception himself while living in Houston with his girlfriend for four years … same case with me, I guess. He spoke about me to his sister Surah and Sam made sure that we bonded too. So Surah and I are in touch with each other. Sam spoke to and emailed my sis too. Sam and I are online almost every day – Issy, he is so good looking and really knows how to treat a woman.'

I just couldn't control my happy emotions anymore – with a laugh I added, 'God, how do you understand your Scottish man? It's so difficult, he's got such a strong accent … he calls me his sexy voice by the way. I know half our lives will go into teaching each other to speak the right accent, but who cares?

'I know it's very important to see each other first and he'll be coming down to Melbourne; I'm definitely not having an online wedding, though he has proposed to me online, but before tying the knot it's so important for us to spend some time together. He already left for Greece yesterday and should be calling me soon. He works on an oil rig, though he is fed up with working on the oil rigs and reckons he is wasting his Oxford degree, so why not put it to the best use? He wants to start his own business. He plans to wind up his work in Greece by the first week of October, it's already the twenty-sixth of September.

'And guess what, Issy? He's coming down to Melbourne for my birthday, on the twelfth. So when he's here we'll get to know each other. He's already taken my passport details, as the laws in the US are quite different: he has to acquire a marriage license, which he has applied for. So let's see. My sis has gone mad wanting to start with the preparation. I told her to hold her horses till we meet.'

It was a bit tough explaining to Issy that my sister had a few issues previously with buying the whole online romance between

Sam and me, until they spoke to each other. 'You have no idea, Issy! I've once again started to dream the dream.' I laughed my heart out.

A patient Issy on the other end of the phone went hysterical on hearing this too. 'Aah, I'm worried about the sex side of it. How …?'

Interrupting Issy, I managed to say while laughing away, 'Don't worry, we will take care of it … online.'

With loud chuckles, Issy finally managed to gather her wits and then in a serious tone she began. 'I hate to be a party pooper … I know … I know it's all good. But he is from online. I'm just worried. I've heard and read so many appalling details about cyber-crimes and the risk of online dating, that you cannot begin to imagine.'

I sensed her concern; I felt that I needed to defend myself but remain polite. 'Issy, as I told you before, sometimes it takes a wink of an eye to fall in love with someone, and you've found your Mr Lovely Buns online …'

Issy interrupted me here. 'Ninty, though Sam is online, he is not here in Melbourne.'

'Yes, true – so was Amit, and what chances did I have after three years, after all the lies and deception? Maybe it's fate, maybe it's destiny, but I've never had so much affection showered on me by anyone before. Remember Sudha, the Indian chick I was working with, who just went through her mind-boggling divorce? She caught her husband red-handed cheating. She didn't waste one moment in seeking a date and now she's planning another wedding. Same site, Issy.'

Issy didn't know that I had confided in Sudha about Sam and she had also told me to be careful. By now, I was pretty exhausted and realised that it was already an hour since I'd come back from the office; I needed to turn on the lights, as it was getting dark outside.

'Hmm,' said Issy, 'I know where you're coming from … have you mentioned this to Shalini and Annette?'

I'd feared this; for a moment, there was silence. Shalini was our ex-manager; Issy, Annette and I worked under her. Over the period of my secondment, I'd become very close to these ladies; Shalini was from a Catholic Sri Lankan background, while Annette had recently migrated from South Africa to Australia with her family. We totally lived up to the statement that Melbourne is a multicultural city. We clicked instantly; when we took to different directions within the company, we made sure that we all met once a month for a movie or for lunch for a good catch-up.

Realising what I was just asked, I didn't want to be rude and bluntly say 'no'. I didn't want to say any more at this point, as at the back of my mind something was bothering me. Was I in denial, not wanting to acknowledge everything Sam had earlier confided in me? I couldn't get my head around it; everything was going too fast. I was also being very superstitious; I didn't want to spread the news, as I was quite embarrassed about my failure with men – it could send out an alarming bell of judgment.

I chose not to ridicule myself and didn't want Issy to know this, so I simply told her that I was waiting for him to come to Melbourne and was being superstitious about the whole thing. However, it didn't take much time for Issy to persuade me to break this news to Shalini and Annette, or for me to persuade Issy to be the initial messenger of this good news. However, I promised, I would email them the next day.

We discussed the wedding, as Sam and I were planning a simple wedding in the temple with very few close friends and relatives. Sam left all the wedding plans to me, as he was living alone in Houston and the only family he had was his sister Surah, who lived in England. He was quite ecstatic that my family had no qualms with having a Caucasian in the family; he respected my culture and wanted to go with an Indian wedding. Once we were in Texas, we would have a church wedding.

As Issy and I often discussed weddings, I had educated her on Indian weddings – how they could be quite ostentatious with lots of colours and lots of attitude. Issy always maintained marriage was not her cup of tea (once bitten, twice shy). I always involved her in my dreams and wove her into my gorgeous wedding, filled with colours, happiness, flowers, food, beauty, henna art, dancing, and lots of music and attitude. She would always see the wedding through my eyes and like a true dreamer, whenever we discussed this, she would say with a laugh that between the bronzed bodies and olive skins, the only one standing out would be her pale white skin draped in a shimmering sari.

I was happy that my conversation with Issy ended with vivid images of my wedding, which was just a flight away from turning into a reality.

***

Isabelle beamed in a beautiful red chiffon sari that had millions of tiny little silver stars woven intricately all over. While she flitted around with the sari, the bright spring sun hit each of those tiny little intricate stars, sending out spectacular glitterati screaming for attention. I saw her mingling with the crowd, blending in – she looked happy. I called her name, 'Issy!'

She turned around, smiling at me. 'Wake up, Ninty, pick up the phone.' Her voice suddenly faded in the background with the noise of the phone ringing, growing louder and louder.

I switched on the bed lamp and looked at the time on my phone. It was 11.30 at night, six hours since Issy and I chatted. I quickly jumped off the bed, as I was sure it would be Sam calling.

A shaken voice came from the other side of the phone. 'Na … Nan!' There was a moment's silence and then Sam began again. 'Nan, I'm in deep trouble, I was robbed at gunpoint on my way to the hotel from the airport, and they took everything, everything – my laptop, my cash … Nan, I was in the hospital!'

I was absolutely shocked, cold sweat running down my face. Surah and I had been discussing earlier that evening that it was highly unlikely Sam would call. But then, he was a grown up boy, he could look after himself.

My heart racing, I said, 'Sam, are you okay? Oh my God, how did this happen, how?'

'I don't know, maybe someone knew I was carrying a lot of money. I don't have anything anymore, just you and Surah.' He let go of his guard this time and started sobbing.

I was trying my best not to sound too dramatic but I managed to say, 'Sam, it's okay, it's only money, as long as you have your life you can earn – most importantly, you're alive.' Deep inside I was silently praying and wishing, 'Please don't ask for money from me Sam, please!'

Losing myself in all sorts of thoughts, I was soon interrupted by Sam's voice. 'Nan, you're right, all I have is you guys.'

'Have you spoken to Surah? She was very worried about you. I spoke to her this evening.'

'I did and she has been very upset, I'll call her again now.'

I felt helpless as I couldn't do anything, but at the same time, I felt I had to be on my guard. He hung up, leaving me restless;

I needed to talk to someone. It was twelve in the morning; both Issy and Sis would be in deep slumber. I called Surah.

Hearing a male voice in the background on the other end of the phone left me flustered. 'Sam, is that you? Hello! Sam! Is that you?' The phone was disconnected. I began talking to myself: 'What the hell was that? Was that Sam?' I may have been exhausted but I could never forget a voice.

I decided to wake up my sis. While narrating the entire story to her, I decided I could have been overreacting, as it had been late and the news must have left me emotionally drained. However, something wasn't adding up. I was tired, that was true – but the voice, I couldn't forget his voice.

In the silence, all I could hear was my own voice in my head – then the phone rang again. It made me jump out of my skin.

It was Surah. 'Nan, did you hear about Sam? I'm so worried, he's lost all his money and belongings. I don't know what to do!' I heard Surah crying softly; it didn't bother me, as I had a question to ask her first, which was burning me inside.

'Surah, I called you, is Sam there with you? I heard his voice.'

'No! Why?' the answer came direct and fast.

'I called you and it was picked up by a male voice, it sounded like Sam.'

'No! No, it was my boyfriend,' Surah replied. The sobs suddenly grew louder. Strangely enough, I wasn't buying any of it. Surah said, 'Sis, Sam needs your help!' Realising what she was about to ask me, my mouth went dry; my worst fears were about to come true. 'Sis, Sam didn't know how to ask you as he was quite hesitant, but I called you on behalf of him. He urgently needs ten thousand dollars to get him out of this mess. I'm sending five thousand, if you could help with the balance?'

Everything around me was slowly melting down and her voice came in slow motion; I thought someone was playing a terrible joke on me.

Issy's words rang in my ears – but then, all this could be true too. Was I overreacting? I could've been, but I always go with my gut feeling and this situation was no exception. I had been wrong in the past and to make my present right, I had to take chances. I decided to go with her story. 'No, no! It's okay asking Sam to give me a call, he shouldn't be hesitant.'

'Exactly, that's what was I trying to explain to Sam, as you and him are not different anymore, we're family now … I will tell him to get in touch with you.' There was no more anxiety in Surah's voice.

Just then it clicked: how were the brother–sister duo in contact with each other when I was unable to reach the former?

Surah hung up; by now it was three in the morning and I was getting pretty tired with the cat and mouse chase, giving me conflicting signals about the whole scenario.

Sam called again. 'Nan, I'm very embarrassed about the whole thing but I need the money so badly, Surah is already sending me five thousand and I need another five thousand. I will sign any paper you want me to sign but I need the money, please.'

'Sam, I understand your predicament but please don't misunderstand me here: as much as I want to help you, I don't have any money to help you. I'm so sorry Sam, but I really cannot.'

There was a long silence on the end of the phone and he began sobbing again. 'Nan, this is for our future. I'm asking for this money as a loan from you so that I'm able to pay the contractors to start my own business. The whole purpose of me coming to Greece was for my business!'

'Sam, I don't have any money, please believe me. I'm on a salary, I just paid my bills for the month. I'm so sorry.' I was adamant by now. I tried to divert from the subject, and was now very inquisitive of his whereabouts. I started questioning myself again!

The persuasion was sounding more like begging and I was getting annoyed. Somehow, I ended the conversation with a false promise that 'I will try'. Tick! Tock! Tick! Tock! There was the time bomb of suspicion, mocking me, warning me of a huge storm surfacing on the horizon.

***

The next day, after deciding not to go to work, the first person I called was my sis. I narrated to her the entire saga of the night, though she was cautioned by my brother-in-law that when money gets involved, it's a dirty game.

I had a few hours left to meet my deadline for Sam. To me it was history repeating – though Amit never forced me for money, he just asked. With Sam, I felt I was being forced. However, the deadline was to arrange a bank loan to pay Sam, so he could pay the contractors for our secure future. I had to buy time from him for my own sanity. I lied!

I didn't realise that this little white lie was soon to become harassment for me. I was overwhelmed, my own stupidity caught in between my emotions and practicality; I was driving myself mad. Maybe in the back of my mind I didn't want the fairy tale romance that Sam had woven into my mind to end; I didn't want to lose him and was still thinking that I was wrong about him – maybe he really was in need of money. I tried to put myself in his shoes, but then I just couldn't add up a lot of things: the voice I heard when I called Surah, her calling immediately after I hung up, her asking me for money and then Sam crying poor with me, all after not being able to contact them. I decided I would call Issy.

'You are not paying him! Are you?' Issy asked me bluntly. 'Though I can believe that this could happen in Greece or anywhere in the world, it's just not safe to travel anywhere anymore.'

I agreed with Issy's statement but I did something terrible: I kept my arrangement with Sam a secret. I was defending the same Sam I wasn't sure about anymore. I wanted to be completely sure of my hunch – and I wanted to save myself the humiliation. I said that Surah was covering the entire sum and he had gone to the police. I hid all my suspicions about the voice I heard when I called Surah.

'Well then, as long as he didn't ask you for money then all is good, keep me posted.'

Surah called again that morning; it was 11.30. I told her that I had just organised everything with the bank and they would inform me sooner if I had been successful. To my surprise, I was able to sell her the idea pretty well and was nervous that I would be seeing either the end of a beautiful fairy tale, or the start of a dangerous game of extortion.

My time was up; it was three in the afternoon without anything in my stomach except a glass of juice, and I was blankly staring at the ceiling when Sam called. 'Hello my sexy voice, how are you? Just called to see what is happening – as of now it's only you, me and Surah. Has something been arranged?' Sam was again at his best with smooth talking.

I decided to lay the cards on the table; I had to stop this, once and for all. 'Sam, I hate to say this, I'm so very sorry, I hope you can forgive me … but the loan got declined. I'm not able to help you at all. I'm so sorry, I don't have any money.' I was about to break down on the phone.

'What? What will I do now? How will I cope? Where will I get the money to give to the contractors?' Sam was now screaming at me.

I was now angry; I managed to tell him to keep his cool and that the contractors would understand his situation – and as Surah was sending him five thousand, that would help him out for the time being. I told him to go to the American consulate to get help if he had to go back to the States. I asked him why he was carrying so much cash. And then it struck me what a liar he was. A passenger needs to declare in customs if he or she is carrying more than ten thousand US dollars. Was I that gullible?

He hung up in anger and I was appalled by this attitude. It was just ten minutes before the phone rang again and this time it was a sobbing Surah on the other side of the phone – she was hysterical.

I said that I was sorry I couldn't help her brother and she kept on like a broken record, 'Save my brother!' I was absolutely shocked when she asked me to ask my sister for money. There it was, out in the open. She blew her own cover, confirming all the doubts already sowed into my mind. I was finally convinced that this was no hunch, that all this was practically a big setup. I never heard from Surah again after that day.

I prepared my sister for the possibility that this brother/sister duo would call her crying for money, and to my worst fear they did. The whole night, I lay in disgust with images of all our emails and conversations. The beautiful love letters, the dedicated love songs, him calling me angel – all shattered in one blow.

Is money everything? Don't emotions mean anything to people anymore? What about the love that he wove into me? Is it so easy to say 'I love you' these days? I could've understood if someone could be infatuated with someone, but this was different: here, two people acknowledged each other about their feelings. Was I so stupid that I turned myself over to him before doing some homework?

The next morning, I emailed Issy everything; she was a little shocked. She told me she'd been suspicious of the story of being robbed in Greece, that sooner or later it would unfold into something like this. We decided to talk later that evening.

My work was suffering and I couldn't concentrate on anything except anticipating what would happen next. I was a walking zombie; the happy attitude was taken over by confusion. I began to hate everything around me.

I rushed to open the door of my flat with my keys, as I could hear the phone ringing; I ran towards the bedroom and I knew it would be Issy. 'Oh my God! Do you realise the name Surah is the name for the chapters in the Koran?' Issy sounded hysterical and nervous. For a split second, I had no idea what to say or how to react – it could mean anything. Then she continued, 'Okay, leave that, it could be pure coincidence as people have exotic names these days, but what about the stories? I'll give you this website, "The dangers of internet dating". Read it!'

As I was going through the article page by page, in the background Issy narrated a story from the same site: a man fell in love with a woman in two weeks and brought her to a world of romance, quickly introducing her to his son. Then he cried for money as he had lost his job.

I was half-listening and half-reading, my eyes travelling from one story to another – I'd been given a key to Pandora's box and wanted to soak up every piece of information. Issy continued her narration in the background: scams, identity fraud and how to spot red flags.

Then something caught my eye: a man from Scotland who would say that his parents were politicians and died in an assassination. I hadn't disclosed this to anyone, but Sam had told me exactly the same thing just a few weeks earlier: how his parents were assassinated as they were politicians, and he kept his mother's maiden name to protect himself and his sister. How he chose to live in England and then fly to America. This was the secret he had confided in me. Now I knew why I was so nervous in the back of my mind, which was keeping me from disclosing it to Annette and Shalini.

'Holy shit, I'm in love with a scammer!' I laughed out loud. I think Issy was surprised with this ridiculous behaviour of mine – soon she joined me and we pissed ourselves laughing for a while.

We continued reading the site; the next thing that startled me was that scammers had a unique way of operating. It wasn't always the same person online; more than one person could be communicating through the same identity. The language and the moods change in each email or conversation. A cold shiver ran down my spine and I could feel the goose bumps in my hand. Images of Sam ran across my mind, his emails and then his voice.

Then we read about the Nigerian scams, where you can trace its fraudulence by the use of language and grammar. They will set themselves in our mind as well educated, highly qualified professionals, but after a few emails when they're refused the money they become hostile, and that's the end of all professionalism.

Issy hung up to do more research, leaving me with a pile of questions. How, when and why? So, fairy tales exist only in books and in our minds – there is nothing called 'love, thy will be done'. Everything is for sale these days. Sam was putting a price on his love.

I threw my hands on my face and then had to remind myself it was not love; he was only doing his job too well.

I was reading all his emails to trace some gaps but that son of a bitch was too good at it. There was nothing that alerted me – a well written movie script. I lit up another cigarette to trace more clues and then the phone rang.

'Hey! Have you got the laptop on?' asked Issy.

'Yes!' I replied.

'I've sent you an email on how to trace someone's host IP address. I'm sure you still have his emails there with you.'

'Yes I do.' Issy had sent me a link on how to trace the location of the sender. All I had to do was copy the defaulted addresses on the page of the link sent by Issy and hit enter.

The results were shocking. The emails were traced from all over Europe and America. The IP traced from Germany, England, and further to Sunnyvale, Dallas and Detroit. I became numb.

I called up Issy to share my discovery in horror; we tossed a lot of ideas through our heads. One of them was he could be a terrorist, or he could have been part of a bigger organisation or a gang involved in human trafficking, or maybe just a computer-savvy thief who made a living out of fooling lonely women. I quickly realised that all these accusations had to have solid proof.

Issy advised me to stop all contact with him but I wanted to pursue it further. I was still strong but withering inside, because destiny had played yet another joke on me. I would not give up the fight for what was mine, and my belief. Nor would I stand the blasphemy of betrayal in the name of love. It had happened to a lot of women – mine was not unique but it also wasn't common. I didn't want to stop all contact with him, either – I wanted to fight this. I didn't want to tell Issy that deep inside I was scared – not because of what 'he' was or what he could be, but because of what he had of mine. I quickly returned to the site where it had an article on 'cyber-sex'.

Sam called again that night. I was impatient, waiting to hear from him so I could hear his tone and see his body language. I didn't want to do anything foolish out of retribution, but it was the flimsy promise of a woman repeatedly scorned by some chauvinists who take extra pride in calling themselves men.

Without wasting any words, he was quick in asking me to jump online. While online, he didn't make a video call; it was just chatting, and he began with the same salutation: 'Hello my sexy voice!'

I wasn't buying it anymore. I was quick not to give any indication of what I knew so far. As polite as I could be, I confirmed that other than love, I had nothing to give him. I didn't have money. It made him very angry, as if I doubted his situation, but then he was apologetic. He was an old player in this game. He was also ashamed of the fact that he called my sister to gauge the mood of the moment, and that he shamelessly asked me for money. He never gave his hotel number, though I repeatedly asked him; he also kept repeating that all the money he was carrying overseas was hidden in his vests. He was an expert on this, a repeat offender to me.

He typed, 'I have one request please, could you help me with some money? I have some hotel bills to take care of, not much.'

'Humour me!' came out of my mouth. I was laughing. 'You were never in love with me, nor would you have come to get married to me,' I snapped at him, typing away angrily. I didn't feel any remorse or regret. On the contrary, he kept avoiding this. I didn't want to alert him but my anger took it away. 'I don't know which part of the world you're in, England or Germany.'

Realising what I just said, I quickly tried to divert his attention. 'I mean, I don't know what to do?'

He was too quick for me, and in came the words in capital letters. 'YOU WILL NEVER BE ABLE TO TRACK MY IP ADDRESS!'

Those letters sent back a chilling message to me. I wanted to punch him in the face; how could I have fallen in love with such a dog? I hated every moment of it. My hands trembled.

Somehow, I managed to regain my composure. This time I had to act fast without revealing my suspicions; I stuck to my story that he never wanted to come to Melbourne and it was an excuse. Sensing that it was alright for now, Sam asked for money again; he needed to settle his bills at the guest house or hotel he was staying at. *Shameless!* I thought, but to my surprise another part of my brain still wanted to believe that he could be right and the facts were just doubts. I had to be strong and stick to one opinion.

Then I said the most unimaginable thing: 'How much do you want?'

He started with seven hundred dollars and I bargained it down to two hundred. He wanted the money by Western Union and would call me the next day to provide the name and the address where I had to send it. I'd just negotiated with a petty thief for two hundred dollars. Was that the price of love? So cheap!

I felt betrayed and cheated by destiny – but I was to blame because I always looked at the silver lining and not beyond it. With email and words, how easy is it for someone to say 'I love you' and then take advantage of someone's feelings? Maybe I was very transparent; my vulnerability and my loneliness betrayed me, so that all I needed was a petty thief to sweep me off my feet. Maybe I let myself believe that I loved him, as I felt secure to have a man beside me. Was this my middle-class syndrome of 'man and marriage'?

The human mind is very cruel, and very unsettling in how it makes you do the strangest of things. My mind played with me on the love of a con man – a make-believe love that I was gullible enough to accept. Loneliness can be a seriously dangerous thing.

***

It was early October, a week since the footy grand final, the end of the football season in Australia – and it was a week since I last spoke to Issy. It was also a week since I lied to Sam about sending money. I was in the office when I received Issy's message: 'Hope everything is done and dusted.' She was referring to Sam and my contact details being changed.

What she didn't know that I actually spoke to Sam in the morning. He begged me for another chance when I confronted him about…? He was seriously in need of money and he also told me that all these accusations could drive him to do the scariest of things, which I could not even imagine. I was secretly trying to break all contact with him, slowly, without him suspecting, and was trying to change my numbers – but I didn't prioritise it with the phone company as a matter of urgency.

In fact, I chose to tell Issy everything was okay. If he was a smooth operator, I wanted to continue speaking to him and see how far he could go. It was just a silly joke when I actually told Issy that maybe the scammer would change and fall in love with me for real. I had enough pressure in my head – work, bills and Sam – and maybe it came out the wrong way, making me sound like a victim of Stockholm syndrome.

There was no response from Issy and then the office communicator flashed a message. 'Nandita, you need continuous drama in your life and then, when things go wrong, you don't spare the drama.'

I read those words not once but many times; I felt as if life stood still for a while. This was what I'd least expected, but maybe she was right – maybe I do sometimes create drama by involving everyone in my life, maybe I wasn't capable of handling my own business and dealing with my own situations. I resented Issy's statement very much. How could I tell her how important she was in my life? Everything that I could not talk to Sis about, I would confide to Issy – that's how important she was for me. I felt betrayed by everyone, my emotions running high.

Suddenly, I was caught between two inventions of the human race, one of a friendship and the other of a con man. I always welcomed Issy and her problems that she chose to discuss. I hoped she would understand me. By my interpretation, friends and friendship were as short-lived as the men in my life. I replied to her as subtly as possible but sometimes the words written are misunderstood in the age of emails (or, for us, the office communicator).

Later I understood what she meant; she had my best interests in mind. I wrote back to her, with tears flowing, that I was sorry to have pulled her into my misfortunes and my drama – I would refrain from troubling her again!

I left it at that, though full credit to Issy: she must have realised how I felt, as she was apologetic in her reply immediately. But once the arrow leaves the bow, it can never be returned – and once the words seep through a broken mind, it can't be fixed immediately. With my head held low and a painful sting in my heart, I was blaming myself. She didn't understand me and it wasn't her fault, but how could I explain I was scared of Sam? By this time, I was tired of explanations. I wanted to break free from him at the right time, as sometimes the price of love is too deep;

it's too hard to let go of the feelings and the dreams. Maybe one day I would explain this to her.

My mother always said, a person who cannot speak may be mute to the whole world; a mute person does not have any enemies, but neither does silence. I chose to become silent. I had already lost faith in love – and that day, I thought I had also lost dear Isabelle forever.

It was the beginning of the end for my shallow love story and I didn't hear the calm before the storm; all I could hear was the dangerous tip-toeing sound of the devil knocking at my doorstep, and I was all alone.

 VAMP SLAYER

> "We are each our own devil, and we make this world our hell."
>
> —Oscar Wilde

Sitting in the train on my way to work, I looked around to see gloomy faces, nervous faces and happy faces. These were some of the Monday morning faces, hiding away behind a newspaper or a book and trying to forget what surrounded them. Some of us make our way to the office because we have to. For others it's an excuse to escape from loneliness.

I too was guilty of the Monday morning blues; I hid behind the earphones of my iPod, not responding to the world.

Reaching my destination, I got off at Southern Cross Station and walked towards the office; I removed my earphones, thinking of what had happened over the past few days. I distanced myself from a good friend and discovered I was in love with a scammer, although I hoped it was all a bad dream and he really was the Sam he told me he was. I was on alert.

My argument about Sam changed when I received his call on the day Isabelle and I parted ways. What happened to the rulebook? All the articles read about dangers of internet dating? Right! They went out the window. Emotions cloud your mind;

the handsome face of the devil, smiling at you, lures you once again into its web, to the point of no return.

Sam said how sorry he was for feeding my misconception about him. He laughed it away; I could hear his laughter right next to me while walking to work, and turning back I realised it was someone else who had a similar laugh like Sam.

I arrived at the office with all this piled up in my head. Sam's constant calls during my lunch time made me feel uncomfortable, while also making me feel wanted again. I was somewhat relieved that there would be no further demand of money and things could settle. I made my best effort to concentrate at work, but there was something lacking in my work and I was pulled aside by my manager.

I was minding my own business as usual, with Sam's continuous check-ups on me. I felt that maybe Sam was changing. Throwing all my fears aside, our nightly chats happened once every three days.

It was just around my birthday that he called me suddenly in the middle of the night. 'Nan, I'm in the night club and wish … would you come on the phone with me?'

I was now wide awake. In the middle of the night, a man calling from the other part of the world asking me to masturbate could only have the mind of a sick pervert. The reply was swift. 'No! I think I need to sleep – you enjoy.'

'Nan, I'm with a lot of other women here, how would you feel?' I could sense what he was trying to do here, but I was not getting jealous – I wanted to hang up. I said to him abruptly, 'Have fun.'

'Would it make you jealous if I told you I was with a prostitute?' He hung up without any reason. What a sadist!

I had to find a way to get out of this mess. I was strangely jealous. I wanted to talk to Issy but my ego came before my friendship. I felt a lot better when there was no communication from Sam in the following days.

***

Anthea, Susannah, Kiera, Sonia and I called ourselves 'SBS', based on the Australian TV channel that features documentaries and films from around the globe. It referred to our cultural background: Anthea being the Greek goddess, Susannah (alias Sandy) the Oriental beauty from East Timor, Kiera the Mauritius hip-hop beauty, Sonia the alluring Thai and me the expressive eyes from India (often confused for being Spanish).

It was my birthday the following Tuesday; being a Friday, the girls decided on a nice Japanese dinner close to work, and after that some fun at the popular club Silk Road. I chose to let my hair down that night, but still with Sam on the back of my mind. I checked my phone to see if there were any missed calls – there were none.

I hurriedly finished work and ran quickly to the bottle shop to grab a bottle of sweet riesling (very popular with the girls). Anthea could not make it, as she was busy arranging a move to Brisbane for her new job. We had Josie in her place, who also shared her birthday around that time. These girls were very special to me, especially Sandy; she would take me out for salsa lessons and dinner after work. She didn't want me to be alone at night when I was going through a rough patch with Amit and other love story failings. (No matter how hard I tried learning salsa, I could never do the right steps!)

Sandy was a beautiful soul with a cheeky sense of humour. She was once seconded to be my boss and it wasn't a happy camp. She chose friendship over career and quickly returned to her original role to save what was sinking: 'a beautiful friendship'. Though I should mention that it was a stressful job being a boss in my department; being with me was equally challenging. Anthea, on the other hand, was always scrupulous about my men and me; she was a twenty-five year old gorgeous blonde who would always be supportive. We would share our painful stories about men, giving advice to each other; her world always revolved around beautiful things. She could be very blunt and abrupt. Her straightforwardness was an appealing quality that very few of us possessed. She would always tease me for being Indian, as half the cabbies in Melbourne would always be in her way – and do I need to say it aloud? They were all South Asian.

I came to know the Thai beauty Sonia through Sandy; they were good childhood friends and neighbours. Sonia was very charming and men would often melt from her soft attitude.

Kiera, the youngest of the lot, was oozing with confidence and no one could escape from her sharp wickedness.

Being the oldest in the camp, I always felt a sense of youthful delight with them; they thought I was a 'responsible person', but they didn't know age doesn't make a person mature or responsible. It just adds a number. Similarly, friendship is not based on age; it is based on how many milestones we cover together.

I was quite excited and felt like a little girl experiencing a sense of freedom when the school rings its final bell for the day. I felt happy after a long time. The girls were all waiting when I turned up. I was happy to be in their company, because there was no discussion of Sam and there would be no gossip revolving around my life. The girls didn't know about him – just a hint of someone I was dating overseas. I decided to be very discreet.

At the Japanese restaurant we had the teppanyaki grill; we started grilling some delicious chicken teriyaki, beef and some greens and fungi on the grill at our table. I munched on some greens with steamed rice, as I'd had far too many glasses of wine that hit me straight up. Maybe it was all I needed.

After a scrumptious dinner and becoming absolutely lightheaded, the girls surprised Josie and me, with a mango cheesecake. I was more excited to just look at it than cut the gorgeous cake, which was making me spin with excitement. After the happy birthday cheers and blowing out the candles, we all dug in to the gorgeous mother of all gluttony, the full-fat cheesecake.

It was already 8.30, and we were busy cherishing the delightful cake and the wine. Sandy announced that she would be booking a hotel room for all the girls to dress up for the upcoming annual office Christmas function. 'Are you in, Nani?' I nodded in response.

Soon we went into the shallow business of what we'd be wearing, and I felt a distinct urge to dig into my dream with Sam – a dream I once thought would be reality. For a few seconds I drifted, thinking about him and me together – slowly realising that I was travelling in unknown territory, falling in love with a scammer. I briefly chuckled at this thought – perhaps it was my intoxicated state of mind. I looked around at the happy faces of the girls, all smiles and laughter without a care in the world. I was jealous.

'I don't know what I'll wear, but something nice,' I said.

Sonia pointed out to me, 'Nan, have you lost weight?' I smiled at this – with the past few weeks, food was the last thing on my mind. I brushed away the comment, as it should have made me happy but in reality I was saddened by it. Sonia's statement had all the elements of a tangled necklace that could snap at any moment.

It was almost 9.30 when we finalised the bill, realising it was too early for us to head towards Silk Road. We decided to take a stroll into the city. It was a balmy night and we checked out a few bars, continuing on the subject of what we should all wear, when Sandy declared, 'Let's all dress up to the maximum as it'll be our last party without Anthea.' We all nodded with approval.

I decided, *That's it: no more feeling sorry for myself.* I'd enjoy the beautiful night and plan the big party that was coming.

By the time we reached Silk Road, it was busy and a huge queue of Friday night revellers stood outside. It was a popular club among all age groups; a mixed crowd but highly distinct. We were welcomed by a gorgeous usher at the door. 'Good evening ladies! Just the four of you?'

We nodded and quickly made our way into the blaring loud hip-hop music. The place was packed; the bartenders were busy taking orders and mixing drinks. All four of us stood patiently in the corner, waiting to be served. Sandy nudged me. 'Nan! Look, that guy's checking you out!'

'Really, where?' Around the corner, just on the right of where we stood, there was a table that was occupied with these two middle-aged blokes; one was Caucasian and the other one would've been of Indo-Fijian descent or something similar. The latter one was beaming at me; I turned my head away. Maybe I was rude. I quickly turned to Sandy, who was giggling away at this scene. I frowned at her and screamed as loud as I could over the music, 'I reckon he is a night prowler.'

'Wha …what?'

'I think he's one of those looking for a one-night stand.'

Sandy just laughed at this remark. I was flattered by the sudden attention from men – it made me feel wanted, but I wasn't interested.

Once we were all settled in a corner, I checked my phone to see if I'd missed any calls from Sam – there were none. After a few glasses of champers, I finally decided to move towards the dance floor with Sonia, who was slowly grooving along with the other revelers.

My whole body was melting away with the music; I couldn't help but laugh like a young girl who had just been introduced to the meaning of 'adrenaline rush'. With my hips swinging, I began to talk like Sam – I never expected 'oh boy' to come from my mouth, sounding like an American. I found it extremely funny, an Aussie-Indian going from the lingo of 'no worries' to 'oh boy'! Was I under Sam's spell?

I was lost in celebrating my life that night; I just didn't care anymore. I danced away. Sandy and Kiera joined in; we gave everyone a run for their money, like we always did wherever we went. Soon people were clapping and joining us; it didn't matter where we were or who was around, we just danced. I don't remember what we were dancing to, but we were just celebrating being friends. It was truly unique and special. I didn't want the night to end.

It was my turn to get the next round of drinks. Crossing the room, I finally managed to get to the bar and returned with two glasses of white, one champers, and one lemon lime and bitters. Kiera was not drinking anymore as she was the appointed driver. I was quickly whisked away by Sandy to 'our' space on the dance floor and came face to face with this tall, lanky-looking hunk with luxurious blonde hair. I smiled and danced a few steps with him. There was no point in taking the dance to the next level, so I quickly excused myself and made my way towards the couch with Kiera.

While sipping my cocktail, I saw from the corner of my eye that Sandy was whispering something to this bloke. He moved sexily towards me, his hips swinging in a fantastic rhythm. I almost burst out laughing and winked at Kiera. He was pointing at me as he walked closer; quickly taking the glass out of my hand, he grabbed my hand and took me into the groove.

'Woohoo!' called Sonia, who could not stop laughing.

Sandy was smiling and quickly came along to interrupt us, pointing at Josie. 'It's her birthday too.' He planted a quick kiss on my cheek and whispered 'happy birthday', looking at Josie. Then we four girls joined him and his friends from England to dance.

I learned that he was working with our business competitor; I didn't care and I didn't want to know anything about him, but it was good to feel good again. Sandy wanted me to get his number but I wasn't comfortable; before I could unleash my flirtiest side again, I pinned myself to the constraint of time. I signalled to my watch and told them it was time to go. It was too early but I was feeling guilty for having so much fun in one night. I thought of Sam on my way home.

It was 12.30 in the morning and I was tossing and turning in bed when the phone rang. 'Nan, I got his name and number for you, he's Brian, do you want the num? Did you have fun tonight, girl?' I could hear the excitement in Sandy's giggling voice and cheering from the girls in the background.

'Yes! For sure I did my darling, now you go and rest up!' Laughing away, I bid them all good night. I knew Sandy's teasing ways.

Reminiscing, I lay wide awake with tears building up. I realised how lucky I was to be surrounded by good friends, even if I was afraid I'd lost Issy.

***

Finally, my thirty-fifth birthday was here, to remind me of all the milestones I had conquered and the failures that came along with them.

After receiving wishes from around the globe from friends and family, I finally got a call from Sam. He was supposed to be here today. I was amid my morning prayers when the phone rang. 'Happy birthday, so what are you doing?' The words came out as if he was doing me a big favour. He hurriedly hung up, saying he would call back again.

It was my day off and I decided to take a stroll in the city to have every moment of the day alone. I visited a jeweller's store, looking at the colourful beads and the beautiful pieces I felt like buying – but I refrained, as I had rent to pay as well as everything else that was needed for survival. I had to make an exit, as I had to catch up with my sister for lunch.

On my way I thought about Sam; he would've been here and we would've met. There would've been a wedding; I would've lived happily ever after. I made a pact with myself not to be sad today, not to cry, not to be remorseful – but to be happy.

The typical Melbourne weather was reflecting my somberness. The cloud would break into rain any moment.

On the way, Sam called again and this time he sounded mellow. He was concerned about how I was coping and seemed very empathetic. I found an excuse to remind him that he would've been here and we would've tied the knot by now. He totally ignored me. I asked him if he would come online so I could cut a small piece of cake with him; his reply to this suggestion was cold. I hung up without any hesitation.

Lunch with my sister was good; it felt like a long time since our childhood together with our brother, with whom we had an estranged relationship. Why do people change after marriage? Or is it the way we think in India? A society that is dependent on sons, a society which rides on the pragmatic belief of the son being the crowning glory of their dynasty. I fail to understand. Perhaps I found comfort in not discussing this, as I believe we waste many precious moments in search of a bigger happiness, forgetting what we have in hand. I was chasing Sam and in that chase, I let go of all the little moments of happiness that made me as a person.

Slowly walking back towards the station with a bouquet of flowers, beautiful presents and cards from my nephew and niece, I began to be dictated by time again. I didn't cut a cake. I wasn't sad to let go of this tradition today – nor was I screaming for attention in my thirties – but I was sad because I thought Sam would have obliged my small, sincere request. It was just another day, just another routine on the calendar. It wasn't special anymore, just another sad love story.

But my circumstances were evidently my call. I could blame Sam but at the end of the day, my own love story was my own shackling, and I had given the keys to Sam. The guilt was too much to be subdued and it never gave me the concession of remorse either. I felt trapped!

I picked up the phone to call my sister when I found a voicemail left on my phone. It was Issy, wishing me a happy birthday. I felt sad that no matter what had happened between us, she was a true friend and I was too stubborn to let go – should I call this ego? No, it was not my ego! But then, my ego would always be pointed out by my family whenever I had to prove my point. I would always be brazen enough to resent what I thought was not right. My opinion would always be blown out of proportion – even though there wasn't always a difference of opinion or conflict of interest.

However, with Issy, it was not ego; it was my expectation for her to ignore all my ignorance. We humans always hear what we want to hear, and sometimes we get too caught up with our pride – then the truth gets pretty tough to handle. Perhaps this was the only truth that divided me from Issy: my own righteous pride!

***

It was a week since my birthday, when I'd last heard from Sam – no phone calls or any reply to my emails. I viewed his chat room profile, and was quite distraught to see the number of women he was suddenly associated with. It was interesting that he'd met with a Thai woman just a week ago – that frankly left me in a loop! I immediately sent him an email, confronting him. There came a prompt reply: 'Have you gone out of your mind?'

This sudden indignation and outburst was very hard to digest and this time I took a different route. 'Well! Then it's all true then, you don't love me after all. What can I say? It was always money.'

'What the hell are you talking about? It's not that, I don't know what you saw so just shut the fuck up.'

The prompt reply from Sam made me shiver; how could someone just play along with such a white lie? It would've been better if he honestly told me that it was a new friend.

I had let go of my suspicions to give him a chance – perhaps I didn't take this into account, that we weren't accountable to each other. Then why was I jealous? The only question that was eating me over and over again: 'Why am I still in love with him?'

I was crying when another email came in. He wrote out of context that as much as he wanted to be with me, he wouldn't be getting any holidays. The email was odd (but so was he) and I didn't want to pursue this topic anymore.

I was packing my beautiful crème sequin dress for the office party and realised that it would fit me perfectly after losing three kilos in two weeks. After work, I'd meet up with the girls in Swanston Street, in a hotel arranged by Sandy, where we would get ready to join the party. It was a formal dress code and I decided to make an effort to look good and enjoy the night.

At work, I was pulled up again by the manager for not delivering what was asked of me and, of course, had to face the consequences.

It was almost five in the afternoon when I checked my phone to see if there were any messages from the girls (there were none) – but there was an email. I opened the email thinking about Sam, but the sender was marked as 'Vamp Slayer'. I thought it to be junk and decided to delete it, but then for some reason I decided to read its content. I was shocked to see it was addressed to me.

Hello Nandita,

You don't know me but I know everything about you, what you do, where you are. I have all the evidence that will work against you. If you scroll down the email you will know what I mean. If you think that you are smart in tracking my host IP then you can try whatever you want to, but you will never be successful. If you want to play smart then you don't know me, how dangerous I can be, and you won't be able to walk on the streets again, you will be a walking shame.

So I have a business proposition, you pay up three thousand and five hundred Euros and I will give you all the evidence back to you to destroy, and if you play it smart then I have no choice but to release the first few tapes to social networking sites. So without any delay I want your prompt reply.

I have given you my mandate and if it is not met in the next twenty-four hours then you will see what I can do.

Reply to me and I will tell you the next step to take. Take this seriously or else live to face the consequences, as I am dangerous.

Yours Sincerely,

Vamp Slayer.

I went cold at this chilling email; my mouth went dry and I could hear my heart thumping. I was lost for words. I looked around and realised I was still in the office. Wiping the sweat from my forehead, I decided I had to put on a brave face. It could be a hoax or a serious mistake – but the email had my name.

I scrolled down and then there it was: a silhouette slowly downloading, then my face, and then the full image of me in the nude. The pictures that I had sent to Sam for fun; those photos were not some copy-and-paste but it was me, they were real. In another file there was a video and I suddenly lost all the courage to see my own self again. It was no joke!

My worst fears were confirmed about Sam. I couldn't breathe; I quickly ran out of the office and felt that I was being watched. I felt naked in the eyes of people walking past me, as if they saw me differently today, judging me like a hated enemy. I was reluctant to walk one more step. I didn't want to go to the office party. I needed to sit and process the situation.

I called my sister. 'It's me … that bastard has done it again! I'm scared, it's beyond explanation.'

My sister was confused. 'What happened?'

As much as I wanted to tell her, I was hesitant about discussing my sex life. I tried to tell her in riddles, but that seemed out of the question. The words came out of my mouth fast like a bullet and sharp like a knife. 'I've been blackmailed!'

'What? What the hell are you talking about?'

Should I be completely honest with her? 'Sunni, I had some photos of mine with Sam and I know it's him, it's him, he's Vamp Slayer.'

'Can you calm down and tell me what has happened?'

I narrated the whole story and in the background, I could feel my voice getting choked.

'How can you be so stupid?'

I wasn't ready for this reply and yet she wasn't wrong. I needed to defend myself but instead I started crying. 'I know! I know! It's my fault, but when you're in love such things happen and I didn't know it would turn out like this. I didn't know Sam could go to such extent, but Vamp Slayer is Sam.'

'Listen, don't cry – you are not a big celebrity that'll be recognised, these days anyone can copy and paste your photo, it's not new. You don't have to tell *Jiju* (brother-in-law) anything, just go straight to the police station. Just go now, lodge a complaint and let me know.'

I still didn't get a solution to my problem; all I got was family pride and hidden agendas.

I stood in front of the tram stop with all my gear for the party. I had six missed calls already from the girls. Should I go to the police station now or should I just go to the party? I was scared and it seemed history was repeating again with me. Just nine months ago, I had to go the Prahran police station to get away from another ex-boyfriend, Amit, and now Sam. How many men would it take for me to learn my lesson, how many? Would there be any end to this insanity? In a rape, the rapist knows his victim, always choosing its prey and attacking like a coward. Today, Sam or Vamp Slayer – the name didn't matter anymore, they were the same – had the same intentions but a different approach to abuse my feelings.

The blood stopped flowing to my veins and my legs froze. I wanted to take a cab to the police station but I had to talk to the girls. I didn't want to be alone either.

Sandy was waiting for me at the hotel foyer. 'Hurry up Nan, we're already late.' I managed a smile and controlled my emotions. Once in the room I quickly ran to the bathroom and shut myself in, putting the shower on so no one could hear my loud sobs.

I quickly managed to change and then one by one, the girls walked in. 'Girls, I think I've made yet another terrible mistake.'

Anthea turned to me. 'Boy trouble again? Nani, I hope it's not *him* again.'

She was implying Amit. I shook my head. 'It's from America!'

We all got ready to hail the waiting cab downstairs. Everyone teased each other in the cab; they looked happy and wanted to talk about everything. I was uncomfortable and I felt naked – I was smiling because they were smiling, I was talking because they were talking. I just didn't have anything to look forward to anymore.

I went outside quickly as I needed to catch some air. The glass of wine didn't help me out at all – it just got me started. I kept my mobile away and ate everything that came my way. The yearly awards were starting and I knew I had to dash out before I got too caught up in the world of awards and banking ... I took a huge gulp of wine and ran towards the door to hail a cab, bidding my goodbyes to the girls as I ran to the streets.

I quickly opened the door to my flat and ran into the dark bedroom. I quickly turned on the lights, stripped and put the shower on full, the cold water leaving me shivering – with that came the tears, the sobs, and the scream. The cold water dripped from my hair and body; shivering from the chill, I fell flat into the bathtub naked. The numbness subsided, but the pain began to take the form of tears. Soon my body reacted to the chill of the fresh air from the window screen of the bathroom. The legs moved, the arms slowly rose to grab the towel, and I collapsed, my whole body numb and heavy.

Somehow, I managed to get up and reach the bedroom to warm myself with the heater. The entire episode of the day began to settle. I had been outplayed by Sam in this dumb game.

Night drifted into daybreak. I refrained from drifting into any more incriminating thoughts, and all I could do was just pick up the phone and inform Narelle that I wouldn't be coming to work – but things got out of control and in the heat of the moment, I said something I shouldn't have said to a manager. The words came out bluntly and quickly: 'Narelle, I've been scammed, my spirit is broken today and it shall never be mended!'

'You okay? What happened? You sound stressed.' A worried Narelle heard the entire story and just kept referring to me as 'poor you, poor you'! I felt validated by her sympathy. I may have sounded like a recluse but I had lost all feelings of human bonding. Suddenly, everything came crashing down in that moment of truth. Amit came in and out of my thoughts.

Had I inadvertently lost everything? Was I still in love with Amit or was it a way to escape him that had brought me close to the edge of losing everything? I was confused and I had no way to seek any answers. I was lost again.

The map of my heart is lost within this silence. Today the heart is a mere part of the body which only beats to live, to survive.

THE POLICE FILES

"Courage is knowing what not to fear."

-Plato

The phone rang continuously. I rushed hurriedly into the bedroom; to hear Sis on the other side made my heart fill with gratitude. I cried profusely and then a decision was thrown right into my face. 'Go to the police station. Tell them exactly what you need to tell them and do exactly what they say. Come on, get out of that house and go straight to the police – you've got to do it for yourself.'

I felt her anger was justified and I knew I had to do something about it. I felt timid walking the streets that led to the police station, as not long ago I had to take an intervention order against Amit – how could I justify this to myself again? It was not only the embarrassment that began sowing doubt in my mind, but it was also the trajectory of my life.

I laughed aloud hysterically. When things go wrong, we seem to blame the universe, the planets, the gods and people, while we forget the silver lining. Still, guilt extends far beyond the truth. It could not be justified; the mind cannot comprehend that the spirit is broken. It still tries to live in a false hope that nothing has changed.

The police station was empty; I walked towards the counter with equal embarrassment and insanity. I rang the bell, and there it was again: my life once again open to be scrutinised on a piece of paper, to be read, to be endorsed. The door opened, *cling* it went, and my heart stopped for a while. I saw the name 'Emily' and my heart sank!

I prayed silently she shouldn't recognise me and I tried to make myself squint – I thought, *perhaps I should wear my sunglasses*. Time was up, I had to write the complaint and with my squinted eyes, I was trying to make myself unrecognisable. Instead, not only did I embarrass myself but I felt stupid.

While narrating the entire story, she looked at me strangely. I looked at the walls, the clock and the missing person poster and then, 'Aren't you the lady who came six/seven months ago, is he the same guy?' The words were burning the back of my ears. So, it wasn't difficult to be recognised after all; as always, I had a very unforgettable face.

After the embarrassing introduction and fall from grace, I stopped trying hard to fool myself – no use, I thought. While waiting for the senior constable, the song 'Like a prayer' popped in my head. Golly! I looked from one wall to the other, shaking my head and closing my eyes, but the song would not leave my head.

'Nandita?' I looked up and saw a constable looking straight at me from behind the desk. I was once again travelling into my past, and with that burden my legs were heavy. I smiled.

I narrated the whole story to the constable and he advised me to wait again, until Detective Raymond Quinton recorded my statement. Life has no ending or beginning; it just travels in its own reality, in its own natural pace. Suddenly, the rulebook of life is out of the window and people become hardened to themselves.

Slowly, I got up and let myself into the back office of the police station. I was greeted by a short, dark-haired Caucasian, possibly in his late thirties. He shook my trembling hands and asked me to narrate everything. I not only felt exhausted but wanted the entire police station to collapse so I could flee. That didn't happen and I had to give him my phone so he could check all the blackmailing notes and photos.

I looked at Detective Raymond Quinton from the corner of my eyes while the constable, Adam, was getting the desktop started to record my statement. I felt a bit disdainful, as he was looking at all the pictures from head to toe. I knew he was just doing his job. I lowered my eyes and felt adrenalin rushing to my head to say, 'Run baby! It's never too late!' I started thinking that all this was a huge mistake; I shouldn't have come to the police station at all. It's not only humiliating but sheer madness to let strangers close to your private life.

Just when the phone was returned to me, the detective turned to me and said, 'Look, Nandita, I see these kind of cases every day, I know it's something new to you but believe me, we have seen worse. This guy could be bluffing – the choice is yours to pay him but I don't want you to. Do you have the original email content, have you got your laptop here? I know you've already traced his host IP but would like our forensics to analyse it too.'

I looked at him bluntly and asked, 'Do you reckon I should cut myself from all social networking sites?'

He nodded with a frown, saying that it's not a bad idea for my own safety, but in reality Vamp Slayer could just be bluffing.

'I broke my laptop so unfortunately I cannot give it you, as it has gone for repairs, but I know, I just know that Sam and Vamp Slayer are the same two people. How on earth could he get all my details like this? I'll soon change my contact numbers and I've asked Telstra to change my email address but apparently the one in my mobile still works, so you can still check it?'

He took my phone, saying to give my statement to the constable. Inadvertently, I was dissolving myself in all sorts of thoughts. When I finished giving my statement, the only consolation I got from the detective was that all this happened because I believed myself to be in a relationship.

We were interrupted by Detective Quinton; he had my phone back with him, and said that I needed to get my laptop fixed for further analysis. Just then, the coffee arrived and the first taste was like Heaven; the shame seemed to dissolve with each sip I took.

I was now eager to look at all the emails sent by Sam and Vamp Slayer, as I knew that they were the same person. My hands went into synch with the email section of my iPhone and without being fully aware of it, I sent an email to Sam. The realisation came to light when immediately there was a reply. It read, 'How are you, my sexy voice?' That was it!

I felt sick, I felt angry and I felt betrayed again. How on earth is it possible for a human to be so cruel, mocking people's helplessness? I didn't waste any time in showing the email to the constable Adam, who called Detective Quinton to see this.

'I want you to handle this very carefully and treat this with diligence. I want to keep him in the loop, so do not stop all communications with him – get as much information as you can. The next important thing is for you to get the laptop fixed so we can trace him,' said the detective.

I nodded and signed the statement. I took his card, gave him a smile and thanked him for his advice. I just needed to run away from there.

I was disgruntled by Vamp Slayer, no doubt, but I was angry. I remembered when I walked past Amit a month ago, like we were two strangers. I felt lost for words but I was so pleased to see him. Was it a womanly scorn or was it the sweet taste of revenge that separated us, but also brought the two of us close today, to walk again in two separate directions?

I didn't understand the equation, as I was now in the same dilemma with Sam. It's not scorn, it's not revenge; it's just a mockery of human emotions. I consent to love without realising the hate, I consent to trust without realising the betrayal, and I consent to falling in love without realising the consequences. Life had taught me a simple lesson: love is not a virtue or fall from grace. To us love comes with conditions, and sometimes without affection; it just turns morbid when it's not realised to its potential.

Funny enough, I just didn't consent the full application of life's redundancy on love and on relationship. I didn't see the vacancy, nor the occupants inside the human heart. I just fell in love. Why was it then incriminating me so much?

 # THERAPY FOR LIFE

> "What is pride? A rocket that emulates the stars."
> –William Wordsworth

I kept looking at the email sent by Zoya; it had the contact number of the counsellor. I was timid, even though I'd been in this situation before, when Amit left me stranded. Today, I needed to be told by someone that it was not my fault. My tears on the weekend needed redemption today, perhaps some kind of mediator or interpreter for my situation.

I looked at the watch, saw my desktop, scratched my head – but I still didn't have the strength to call the number. I decided to take a walk.

I walked along the riverside, the cool northerly wind and the sun feeling quite refreshing. Across the river there were cruise boats lining up. A sound came from the background, and I saw a boat full of rowers in sync, rowing back to back with full strength. I saw them almost every day – sometimes in the morning when I was having my first cup of coffee and thinking about the day, sometimes, during the afternoon, as I sat with a box of sushi. They practiced this routine day after day.

It was no different today, but this time I saw something I'd never seen before; they had a unique spirit, a determination not to fail their teammates. They were all listening to the navigator, their hands in unison, their minds not competing with each other as competitors. They were in sync with one another with the same determination: to reach one goal.

'Hello! I would like to make an appointment please!' I said with confidence. I was to see Dr Pam Fraser in the following week.

***

I saw the train arriving at Southern Cross around 5.30, with people trying to find a needle in a haystack. Millions of people would be doing the same around the world, irrespective of their time zones – trying to reach their loved ones, trying to eat, trying to get another day out of their way.

I looked back; standing next to the vending machine, this guy reading a newspaper was actually not reading, but looking at me. This tall, massive big guy leaning next to the bin with the evening paper was actually looking at me. A guy sitting on the bench with his girlfriend whispered something to her while looking at me; now they were looking at me and laughing. I felt cold. My heart racing, I looked at the public screen to check the schedule of the train, then checked my watch and looked around.

To me, the scene was an espionage movie, as if all the real characters were staging a conspiracy against me. I couldn't see a place to hide; I was suddenly naked under those screening eyes, and I remembered Vamp Slayer's words: 'You won't be able to walk on the streets again, you will be a walking shame.'

I wiped the sweat trickling my forehead and inside I prayed, 'This is not real! It's just my phobia, it's just me … me.'

I quickly jumped onto the train, and there I closed my eyes, only to realise my worst fears. As the train crossed the tunnel, finishing its city loop round, the train reached its next destination,

Flinders Street. A blond, tall man with piercing blue eyes sat opposite to me. I guessed he was listening to some music – and then in a fraction of a second we both looked at each other. I lowered my eyes and through the mirror reflection of the opposite side, I could see him taking his earphones out and looking at me. I twitched, it made me uncomfortable, and I looked away.

From the corner of my eyes, I saw he was still staring at me. I had this massive urge to go and slap him but instead I managed my guts and somehow, I looked right back at him. This happened for a good five minutes until the train screamed, 'Next station, South Yarra.'

I quickly pushed the door of the train open and ran with all the strength in my body, as far as I could go. I pushed and stumbled across people; I didn't care if my feet were in agony because of my shoes. I ran as fast as I could towards my flat – when I finally reached it, I just collapsed on the floor and sobbed.

When the tears dried up, when the soul tried to align with the fatigued body, the mind needed some reassurance to relax. I went to the chest of drawers by the bathroom and took out the restraining order; Amit's signature was still there. I drew this line to cut him out of my life so that I could heal myself from his deceits, from his rejections and from him. Strange as it may sound I missed him today, but it was more like I was missing a friend – all I needed was a friend. I looked at his signature again and touched it.

A teardrop smudged his signature; I rubbed my eyes and tried my hardest to wipe the soggy paper. I kept it away, not able to think about that moment. So I went to my diary and there was poetry by Rumi; it was about a friend, on a beloved's return. I felt a bit relieved reading the poetry and wished Amit well, wherever he was.

**

From my sister's drawing room, you could watch a cherry blossom tree that was blooming in its fullest; it was hard to believe that only a few months ago it was bare in the harsh winter. I tried smiling but the dry aura left me wondering about sentiments that had little value today. I wanted to say something that could be transformed into something beautiful, but then I saw this cherry blossom as just a tree. It was highly impartial to the broken spirit.

I left my sister's place with this thought in my heart, when the phone rang – it was Sam. I heard his voice and disconnected it.

The therapist's office was on the sixteenth floor. As the lift sped up, I held onto my thoughts. The lift opened to an unattended reception; I could see the bright spring sun from one of the rooms, capturing the entire room with its power, and the reflection of the sea below on the glass was captivating.

I heard a creak on the glass door and behind it, there was a slim figure approaching me. 'I won't be long, I just have to get a room which is free, do you mind waiting?' I shook my head, focused on what I would be saying to her, but my emotions ran wild and I hardly knew what to say.

'So what made you come to see me?' Pam looked at me sharply from behind her glasses, after I'd sat down in her office. Her nose was pointed and her dark brown hair tied back perfectly in a ponytail. Her three-quarter pants and her black jersey blended perfectly with her office. The room just had one window overlooking the sea and it had one table with a computer. On the wall there was a picture of some kind of flowers. Besides the two couches in the room, there was just this awkward silence. Her hands clasped together, Pam looked towards me and then looked down at the notebook as if she was recording something.

I narrated the whole story, looking out the window as I didn't have the courage to meet her gaze.

She took her glasses off and shook her head. 'Next time you decide to do anything like that, uh-uh!' She made a chopping motion against her neck. 'Chop that head of yours out of the equation.'

The remark combined with her expression made me laugh.

'You aren't naïve to trust someone like that; it's a long-distance relationship and you're bound to do that at some point … not saying that we should always do that, but these things happen. It is love, so we call it!'

I looked at her. 'Pam, I've resigned from my job and I want to go back to India, away from here. Am I running away from the situation? I don't know if it's the right decision.'

She lowered her neck and pulled her glasses up on her head, breaking into a smile. 'You've just experienced a harrowing ordeal and you're confused. Why did you resign?'

I then felt the need to speak to Pam honestly; until now, I was pretending that I had to get back to my roots. I looked Pam straight in the eyes. 'I resigned from that job not because I'm scared of Sam, that he would damage my reputation in any way. All my failed relationships seem to have a domino effect and it seems to have emerged since I started my job there. Am I being superstitious? Maybe I am. I know it's crazy to think that way, but I'm a person like that. I don't know …'

I paused for a while, looking outside the window, the sea shimmering with sunlight. There was a yacht heading somewhere, sailing to or from its destination – I wished I could sail away with it. Perhaps it was a bad idea for me to have come for the session. I was sitting here and pouring out all these inner thoughts.

Today, my private mind was being tested and I was letting it subjugate me. I never let myself close to it until now; in the past, I would turn a blind eye and focus on something happy. It all started with Amit but I never approached the problem until I saw it happening again with Sam. The pattern had to be broken and Pam broke it today.

I guess Pam did read my mind – she had to. 'It's nothing to do with you – if you want to get away from here for a while, not forever, then take the time to heal and then come back. Fair enough if you don't want to work with the bank, perhaps you can come back and join another company. Don't let this overshadow your life. We all have to overcome our doubts to let go of our fear. You will come back and, one day, realise that all this was a bad dream; you have to learn not to regret, but to learn from each experience.'

Maybe these were the words that would actually lead me to my next journey. Perhaps it was not a bad idea to come after all.

***

I was walking towards the bus stop with a sudden rush of adrenalin; the last time I felt like this was when I saw the rowers a couple of weeks prior, before I made the decision to see Pam. Today, the adrenalin was different; it had the rush of life, and it formed my lips into a smile. It was not because of what she said; it was what she verified for me. I knew this all along. I just needed to verify it with someone and I needed to authenticate a long haul of doubts that overshadowed my happiness, brewing in me as a constant nag. I suffered in the hands of my own past and I overlooked that to be suffering in my present. I never despised my own belief to go for the perfect love, but I alienated myself from what I wanted, what I believed in. I forgot myself.

There are a lot of people who cannot achieve a lot of things in life; there are a lot of people who aspire and dream. I dreamt too, but the history of my life got measured against the frailty of my heart. I forgot to be happy. What is it to love and how does it feel to not be loved?

Love is the moment of truth and faith is the moment of solitude – both walk hand in hand when you truly believe in those three precious words: I love you! To me, that's what love is.

THE MOVE

> "You must be the best judge of your own happiness."
>
> —Jane Austen

Across the room, I glanced towards the mess I had created with the clothes and the shoes; a few boxes could not withstand the pressure of the clothes that were sticking out of the sides.

After a trial day of cleaning, I decided to quit the boxes as the pressure was enormous. Each dress I packed, each card I tore, each and every piece of crockery and cutlery that I boxed had an emotional story attached to it: a dinner party, a birthday, a festival, a celebration of a promotion, dinner with Amit, clubbing on Saturday nights with the girls. It felt as if I was folding my life, piece by piece, fold by fold in those dresses, cards, crockery, cutlery, paintings and photographs. Even in the furniture, there was the crease that Amit left on the seats of the sofa, the huge fight we had near the bed, the DVDs he bought me, and the dining table where I wrote to Sam.

My life quietly unraveled in front of me without even blinking and in that moment, everything just looked like a movie gone wrong with a bad script. I didn't have the remote control to rewind or fast-forward; it just had to be played without any retakes or reshoots.

Was I being a child again, who would rebel at anything, even at the slightest thing? I remember when Maa forced me to eat fish curry and rice- I would use all the tricks available in my little magic brain. I definitely thought I was invincible, just like then.

Back at the apartment, I could see the boxes taking up most of the space in the lounge. There wasn't enough room to move around; it felt the same way when I moved to South Yarra, with Amit helping me out. This was no time to go back to the trail of thoughts but I felt my astringent heart again. The entire room looked as if it had been bombed. The irony here was that the same apartment I liked three years ago had now become a hazard for me with stale memories.

***

I looked into my cup of coffee. Was there a storm brewing or was it the emotions churning to break free from the old Nandita, who lost herself chasing after love and relationships?

Reading my mind, Pam cut the muffin in half. 'Here, have this, taste it. What do you taste?'

I looked at her blankly. I didn't understand the question. 'You mean to say what it tastes like, right?'

She nodded. 'Yes! When you put the first forkful of muffin in your mouth, what did it taste like – what is the first thing that comes to your mind?'

'It's sweet, grainy and buttery, yeah!' I said to her.

'Correct! That's my point. You are savouring the taste of this muffin, the same way you have to enjoy life and let loose your fears. You know what to do, Nandita. We can sit here and complain about the same muffin – perhaps the butter should have been beaten more thoroughly to make the muffin fluffier, or perhaps it's runny and tastes very grainy. We can use as many adjectives as we like to make the muffin tastier and more precise according to our tastebuds, but at the end of the day it'll taste according to the effort and the hard work we put into preparing the muffin. So, we can sit here not only to eat and enjoy it, but also so we can analyse it.'

After the visual trip from the kitchen, from the first crack of eggs to the baking tray, I came back to our conversation at the café, at our table where I was sitting with Pam.

That day I realised the most crucial and basic aspect of survival: we forget to enjoy and savour the simplest thing, called life! We take everything so seriously that we forsake the good to be damned by the bad, and then the regrets start to sink in. We forget to savour the moment, as we're too caught up in the future. We forget to let ourselves loose, because we're too conscious of what others might think. We forget to live.

We follow routines to rule our lives just because everyone else is doing so. We set these rules for ourselves because we consider it better if we set boundaries – and we become a victim of our own fallacy. I had to break my rule.

 # AUGUST 2011

> "Every man loves two women; the one is the creation of his imagination and the other is not yet born."
>
> **Khalil Gibran**

*B*efore I reveal my travel and experiences in India from January 2011, I have to write what happened in August of 2011, coming back from India to rebuild my life once again in Melbourne. I was trying to give up on love and its fantasies. Sure, this time the door will be created, a safe haven; but then suddenly God gives you Franklin. You all will understand why I mention 'God' in the next chapters. I can almost tell you in India I was touched by God's life.

Sitting at my dining table in my apartment in Melbourne, it was very important I write this. Sometimes, we all have to travel to our present to see what we've learned from our past – in saying that, it is equally important to travel into the past to nurture the future.

It would be foolish to say that I've attained everything that is there to attain. Wisdom and history bind human life; one cannot live without the latter and we don't stop learning – it's a never-ending experience.

I looked at Harry, my housemate, sitting across the dining table with Brea, his friend. They were talking about her recent trip to America. It was funny, as I was thinking about my past in India.

The previous night, I'd decided to cook for Harry and Brea. I asked Harry (or Prince Harry, as he liked to be called) his permission to write about him. He is six foot three inches tall and to him, sports and music are his life. He has a harem of guitars and names for each one of them. He is a quite a musician too.

I befriended Harry during my last job and we'd been acquainted for quite some time. When I came back from India, I was staying with my sister and her in-laws again. Things weren't easy; not only was it a huge family and things were a bit cramped, but also it was hard for an individual to live by their own rules at thirty-five. I was looking for a place and for Harry, it was an immense task to travel three hours every day from Werribee to the city and back. He reckoned with that time he could travel to Sydney and back, or he could sleep after his rowing session. (Did I mention he is a rowing champ? It was a pleasure for me to meet all his rowing mates at our housewarming.)

He is an Australian born to American parents. His parents came from Michigan to open a church in New South Wales some twenty-nine years ago, when he was born.

So, as soon as I activated my Facebook space after six solid months I was once again connected to the world.

One day I posted on Facebook, looking for a room in a decent suburb in Melbourne and everything else is history. It has been nearly one and a half months since we moved in together. We made a pact: I don't come between his harem of guitars and his beautiful girl, and he doesn't make any moans of passion.

I could live with that. We have an amazing bond, we understood each other's space and we respect each other's company.

The previous night, Brea mentioned that her boss in America, while she was there working some years ago, usually put it across to her, 'You cannot fight fate!' I thought how simple yet how bold the statement was.

I felt as if fate was staring at me, telling me that all that was happening to me is beyond my control. . I believe we're born to live our fate.

To rebuild something that is destroyed is hard. As human beings we still don't give up; we fight against all odds and we seldom trust ourselves – but then somehow, we do. I returned from my time in India across 2010–11 with what I thought I'd lost. I did my share of travelling, of being lost and found in delusions and illusions, but somehow, I found it – or did I? Maybe those millions of pairs of eyes in India each had a story to tell – perhaps through their eyes, I realised what it is to feel and gain again?

Was this some kind of test that I had to pass to succeed in my coming future? Then again, the whole equation of karma and fate becomes unbalanced. While writing this, I realise what I found is infinite but what I lost is rare.

The previous night, I laid awake to the passionate moaning that came seeping through the walls from the next room. It tormented me and the wine that I drank did nothing to liberate my inebriation; in fact, it stimulated me. I was jealous and lonely, wiping the tears that came fast and without any notice. I couldn't do anything to stop them. I tossed and turned and tried to make sense of the past month, meeting Franklin only to lose him again.

I called him Franklin; he would laugh at it. I decided it would be best to keep his identity the same little secret as my falling for him over the coming days and months.

Meeting a man like Franklin upon my return to Melbourne was different and unique from meeting the young drifter – I say drifter because his heart was aimless and never empty – in Delhi, four months prior. My meetings with both these counterparts were unique and something I was not expecting. Vinod is still there and a friend; he was just a silly infatuation.

In Delhi I embraced and understood what love is through a place called The Missing Peace; when Vinod knocked on my door, it felt like the opportunity was mine. In reality, it was not meant for me. He was my fantasy in which I found myself infatuated again.

The universe sends these cryptic messages, testing us to differentiate between love, lust and loneliness. The universe sends these messages to us, but the human heart is too naïve to understand. Then it comes back to the same theory: 'You cannot fight fate.'

At first, I didn't understand this pattern, but later on I did and I would dread this happening. Simultaneously, in the gap of a few days or weeks, the connection is lost – and with that, the man too.

The day I met Franklin was historic for me. When I came back from Delhi I took a job. In the office I saw him here and there, but when I did look at him it was with a very professional glance. I'd bump into him at the café down the block and an exchange of greetings would be our only form of communication. During lunch breaks, Franklin would come down to my floor to play table tennis. Still, nothing happened.

Once, we caught each other staring, me from behind the walls that secluded the lunch area from the play area. I still didn't understand; it wasn't revealed how we were destined to meet, know each other and then separate.

It was a cool Wednesday spring morning, still chilly from Melbourne's erratic weather. I was meant to start late that morning, but without a shot of caffeine I don't function well.

My morning routine started with going to the same café; I'd purchased my coffee and then there he was. 'Are you waiting?' I asked. He replied with a no and moved away from the counter. While we waited for my coffee, he started a unique conversation about my last name; he knew my Bengali origins. I was pleasantly surprised that he knew a lot. 'My name means "happy" in Bengali,' I told him, and he spoke about a Bengali friend in the UK whose name was an acronym of something sweet.

We walked outside and the cold air had made my eyes watery. 'You crying?' I was taken back by Franklin's statement. I shook my head to say no but then he interrupted me. 'It is symbolic!' I was amazed at this, as if he was reading me already or did we meet before? Where? Definitely not in this life.

I went very enthusiastic and spoke nonstop. I was myself again. I saw a grin on his face and when he came to know I was thirty-five, he was shocked. 'All I have is leathery skin and the dimples.'

I laughed and all I could manage was, 'Good genes of the Bengali and their fish-eating.'

He chuckled. We spoke about what I did in the past regarding work and I told him about my recent journey to India and that I was writing a book. He looked at me with curious eyes and mentioned how he wanted to do all that. We agreed on our appreciation of Bollywood films and I gave a brief introduction of my father's films that won him accolades, both in India and overseas.

I looked at my watch and it was time to go. I didn't think anything of this sudden meeting, nor was I aware of the coming storm. I just flowed in the moment. He wanted to be in touch to discuss my book over a coffee or emails.

By then, I had to confess I always knew him, but never his full name; it was always confused with other names. He gave me his full name for email; I had a big grin on my face.

The day started with a lot of research; I found him and emailed him. He replied that great minds think alike. We started with an exchange of our mobile numbers and our deep conversation on Indian films and his liking for Sufi songs. We talked about my book and he wanted to read some part of it. Only if I wanted him to, perhaps over coffee or over dinner.

I still didn't pass judgment as to what this was leading to, just happy about this sudden excitement. We discussed his favourite Indian movie (*Earth*) and how he was almost in love with the actress; I had to make it a point that she shared the same name as me. I got a 'Ha-ha!' back in reply. I told him he should watch *Monsoon Wedding*, as this is my favourite, and promised to give him my DVD.

The day ended in a smile and then the texting started. He mentioned how he discussed me with his Indian friend. I was ecstatic and impressed that he managed to discuss me with his friend in this short moment.

By then I was beginning to debate with myself, how we women begin to over-think beyond any reason. It happened with me recently with Vinod; they can be all sweet talk but I know what it is to feel and not to feel, as I've come out of this conventional, stereotyped mentality.

I reached home and told Harry. He made a quirky remark; if people didn't know him that well, they would call him rude. I took it as good humour. According to Franklin, the greatest romance told is not the greatest unless people die at the end, or kill each other.

I have to say he has a point; some of the best stories, plays or books are all based on these theories. 'Oh dear!' I made a face at him and went into my room.

The next day, I learnt how keen he was to read my book. I realised that my *Monsoon Wedding* DVD was not there, as somewhere during my move to India I had given it away or misplaced it. He told me not to worry, as his Indian friend had stacks of DVDs and he was sure to lay his hands on *Monsoon Wedding* somewhere.

It's not important who asked whom out, as we both were keen to meet. But Franklin initiated: perhaps any time I was free I could just shoot him an email and we could discuss the book over coffee or a dinner?

I was delighted to have found a new friend. I accepted the dinner invitation and it was fixed that we would meet that evening. I had to wait for his call.

Running around my apartment as a headless chook, I got ready for my workout and in the background I could hear Harry teasing me. I just laughed it away. Packing my gym stuff and the first chapter of my book, I headed towards the city. I was happy and determined not to be overexcited with sudden bursts of enthusiasm.

Finally, we met. He had his car and around the city we went. On the city tour I learned he was separated, had a son and was also in love with 'Sweets', his friend in the UK who left to travel overseas; he could have asked her to stay but he was not selfish. He didn't go to be with her because of his love for his son. He showed me the book he was reading and the beautiful bookmark designed by her.

By now, I was telling him my life; he didn't feel like a stranger and he was patient, listening to every word I said. Franklin kept telling me how fascinated he was by me. I must have sounded like a creature from another planet, but that was me.

He told me how he loved the movie *Aarakshan* and a little story behind buying the tickets. He'd called the cinemas to get the show time for the movie and in his own pronunciation, he did his best to say 'Aarakshan' but the girl on the other end of the phone did a superb job of customer service by saying it as 'erection'. We had a good time laughing at this.

We talked about Indian culture, the caste system and how we still lived in a society morally influenced by hypocrisy.

I gave him an example about our Bengali culture and how the '*kumars*' (sculptors) who sculpted the deity, cannot be fulfilled unless soil is brought from the home of prostitutes. It is a ritual that has been going on from centuries, yet it is also a ritual to hate them.

The Goddess Durga is considered a powerful goddess and therefore, the soil from a prostitute is considered to be holy or pure. I would often hear this story when I lived in Kolkatta; each time during the *puja* (prayers) of Goddess Durga when the *kumar* Tulli made the deities, the soil would come from a prostitute's courtyard.

I conveyed this to Franklin from memory. I was grateful to him for the trip down memory lane and secretly thanked him in my heart.

He took me to Brunswick Street, where I had a shop once upon a time, and memories came flooding back. The car came to a halt after numerous debates over where we'd have dinner and circling Smith Street.

'What is love? Tell me Happy, I'm trying to make sense of it all.'

'I know what love is!' I said aloud with great conviction.

'Are you in love?' he asked.

I smiled at him. 'No, I'm not in love but to know what love is, it's not important to be in love with someone. Call me a romantic, but love has many definitions. Look at this, for example: the sun, air and water. They're all free and people say the best things you enjoy in life are free.

'We enjoy them because we love them, not only because they're free but because they're the most beautiful things that have been created. Similarly, love is also between a child and its parent, between a brother and sister, between friends. The whole point of me writing my book is to tell people to believe in love and also to keep the door of their heart unlocked – as you never know who'll knock.'

I later knew that he would be going on a holiday for two weeks and had also bought a surprise ticket for his dear friend 'Sweets' to accompany him in Jordan. For a moment, I thought it would be good if these two beautiful people in love could unite … but then again, love cannot be forced – it has to come from within.

I also mentioned to him I haven't found an ending for my book. At this, he made a smart-arse comment: "Maybe I'll be in the book and you'll have your ending."

I couldn't help but laugh at this attempted sense of humour. I remembered someone saying the same thing to me not long ago: Vinod, in India. It was deja vu.

***

We sat outside this café in Brunswick Street. I can't remember the name; it was his smile's fault. He was quite surprised to learn that I smoked and admitted he was a smoker himself.

We exchanged stories of our family histories over the chef's special fish. Franklin ordered a house red and I was on the verge of ordering my skinny latte; at that, Franklin chuckled. 'Come on, you live only once, have a fat latte.' I nodded, Franklin smiled at the waiter and he said, 'One house red and latte.'

I corrected, 'Fat latte!'

There I was, having the delicious fish and telling him about my brother's distance from the family – he asked me why. I told him it was my brother's choice and a complex thing to explain, but when the time was right, he would come again.

We spoke about my relationship and how I'd forgiven Amit for moving on, and how I was close to my father. 'You look so young and yet so mature.' I laughed at this, not sure how thirty-five year olds were supposed to look.

I excused myself to go to the ladies. The chilly night was refreshing (like him). On my return, I was surprised he ordered a chocolate cake and to my horror, it was a massive piece. 'Here I am, trying to reduce the weight I carried from overseas, the good life and home-cooked meals and sitting on my arse for six months.' He just smiled at this.

Franklin paid the bill and to my repeated insistence he replied, 'Of course you would have paid.' I didn't harp on about it.

I took out the first chapter of my manuscript, neatly placed in a manila folder, and gave it to him. 'This is for you! Read it when you can, not now but later.' I didn't want to sound as if I was obligated to him for the dinner, but the whole point of the evening was to discuss the book. It didn't matter if we discussed the book, but what mattered was that we discussed our lives.

'Are you sure?' he asked.

'I am, you keep it, and it doesn't matter.' I smiled. 'If you try to copy, I will sue you.' We both laughed.

We left the restaurant and walking along Brunswick Street, Franklin took my right arm into his and we walked arm in arm. He said, 'Happy, look at you! Here you are sharing your life with a total stranger.'

To this, I added with a smile, 'Are we?' I tried to say something like, 'Well! You got me nostalgic.'

While waiting for the traffic to clear so that we could cross the road, his arm still on mine, like teenagers we both were giggling. I was amused.

Once inside the car, he was more excitable than before, as if I had infused some kind of life into him. He reminded me of me somehow, how I would react if I met someone nice: I become a chatterbox and very random. Franklin would tell me how lucky he was to have friends who would give him his car to borrow, and his friend who gave him a fully furnished flat for him to stay while she was in London. He gave the house to his ex, so their son could be brought up there – he did this out of love.

I learned that Franklin was a man of humility and kindness, a gentle soul lost in his own translation of love. He was lost but not selfish. In retrospect, we can all be selfish, including myself. He was elusive – but then, which man is not? He was careful but not cunning. He was intelligent but not deceitful.

On the ride home, he was showing me how nervous he got and how his hands were shaking. I touched them and asked why. To this he responded that he gets shaky when he's excited. I smiled.

We continued our chat and I spoke about what a wild one I was, almost the black sheep of my family. He was quite amused. I said to him I felt like getting a tattoo of the word 'recluse' all over. He laughed at this and suggested I should get a phoenix done. He'd already planned a tattoo of a snake and a tiger, their forces meeting a fairy at the fountain and looking at a beautiful baby boy. It didn't take me much time to figure out the snake and the tiger sun signs from the Chinese calendar. He was indeed a man of love.

He dropped me off at my house; he was awed to see how close I lived to work. He was a thorough gentleman; he kissed me on the cheek and left me in front of the building.

Picture perfect. I stood there smiling for a long time.

NEW DELHI – JANUARY 2011

> "I came, I saw, I conquered."
>
> — Julius Caesar

Through the window of my car, I was seeing a new India. Transforming and changing, through its organised chaos, which retained its impeccable beauty.

This was the land of Tagore and Gandhi, where Rudyard Kipling wrote his jungle book – suddenly the jungle was alive. Sadly, the jungle now is that of concrete and Western modernisation. I wondered for a split second what Hollywood would do to make a movie on poverty in India.

This thought made me a little sad – not because Hollywood wouldn't find any subject to exploit the poverty, but I was thinking as a Westerner, not as a progressive expat. I was ashamed.

I wanted to see India progress – but progress is not fine roads and classy cars. To me, it's progress of the mind, progress of people, and no vast difference between the rich and the poor. Then people would argue with me, that people like me run away from all this, so that they can progress for themselves on someone else's land. When they're tired, they return for salvation and lecture on right and wrong.

I felt I wasn't entitled to it anymore. I felt selfish to criticise something that wasn't for me anymore – or rather, that I was yet another Westerner who was jealous of the progressive India.

In two years, a lot had changed, from the airport to the roads, but the honking of the cars was alive and the people ... they were the people who make the biggest democracy in the world.

Suddenly, I was glad to have found my connection; perhaps I would re-introduce myself to its people again. It was crazy to be in love with the sound of horns and to see people buzzing everywhere, still walking on the roads rather on the footpath. Nothing else mattered; I was at peace.

When we reached home it was almost midnight; winter was almost upon Delhiites. I kept teasing my mum that she didn't recognise me as I came out of the airport. I just walked past her and she didn't notice me at all. My short hair seem to upset everyone, as I looked like a boy. They looked at me with total contempt, as if I had chopped their long hair.

While enjoying a hot cup of tea – in my shorts, as I declared I was feeling a bit warm due to the fact that winter in Delhi is not that severe – I felt a mixture of jetlag and nostalgia.

I felt torn between two cultures and two worlds – my life was in reverse mode, walking backwards from my present into my past. It was a feeling of building something – I just didn't know what.

Suddenly, I was angry with myself and with everyone around me. Was I already regretting travelling thousands of miles to India?

I saw it in my mother's tired eyes and my father's smile. They both felt sorry for me and somehow felt responsible. I didn't travel here to gain their pity or sympathy, and not to play the blame game. I wish I could make them understand that I came here to forgive myself – it had nothing to do with them, it wasn't their fault. My wounds are self-inflicted and my sorrows are my own. I just needed to find my own path, my own healing.

I barely touched my dinner and Mum's continuous nagging was kind of nice. 'Here, at least have the dhal and take some rice.' Mum poured some more of her delicious yellow lentil dhal.

'Maa, you can see what I've come to; I gained weight while staying at Sumi's place. I'm here, I'm not running away, so just a little will be fine,' I managed to say while gulping a spoonful of rice in my mouth.

She raised one eyebrow and said aloud, 'Yes! You look like you've put on some weight.'

I just smiled wryly and said, 'Yes! I know!'

The next morning, I woke up to the sound of birds on my window and I saw the crisp winter sun heading my way. I now felt cold and tired. I saw Mum still next to me, as I remembered Dad asking her to sleep in my room with me. I could've said no to the proposal, but I took the offer; I wasn't scared of the dark, but of the journey ahead of me. I needed someone to be with me. Dad making the decision for me was kind of nice.

'What time is it, Maa?' I shook Maa's elbow.

With her eyes half-open, she turned to her side to see the table clock. 'Six-thirty! Go back to sleep, I will get up in a while – great, Rabida and Khokhon are still sleeping.' She called out loudly, 'Rabida! Khokhon! Do we get tea or not?'

I smiled; my mother hadn't changed a bit. That's the beauty of being born Indian: we're loud, unpredictable and seriously dramatic.

Rabida's proper name is Rabi, but we add 'da' as for an older brother or uncle (it's Didi for any older sister or aunty in Bengali). I call him Jethu, meaning 'uncle'. He'd been living with us since I entered the world. He is my dad's cousin and after his wife's death, no one would take responsibility for him. He and his three daughters came out to Kolkata from the country. Ever since then, Dad had been looking after his family, from paying for his daughters' education to their weddings.

Dad at one point was a renowned filmmaker in Kolkata, making many well-known films that won many awards. From the President's Gold Medal to the Silver Bear in the Berlin Film Festival, he had the opportunity then, to do what he did for Rabi Jethu. Now, things were different: now, they all looked after each other.

In the lounge room I could still see one of the prestigious awards, The Filmfare Award Dad had won in 1982. The award is a silhouette of a lady sculpted fully in bronze, with Dad's name engraved on the bottom along with the name of the film.

I looked at the beautiful lady again, the bronze body silently standing after all those years, speechless – moving from house to house, corner to corner, glancing at all of us.

I looked at Jethu's face; age had not been so kind to him. Life had been harsh and the lines on his face were a testimony to this. Still, he would do things without any complaint, always with a smile. He'd been with us through thick and thin, from Kolkata to Delhi.

He normally did the housework these days and helped Mum. He would put any thirty-year-old to shame with his amount of work.

Khokhon had been with us for the last fifteen years. It is a very popular name in Bengali; if you didn't know any name to give anyone, of course it would be Khokhon (sometimes as a pet name). In his case, it was his pet name: his real name is Ekadashi but we called him Khokhon.

He was from a village called Boro Udaipur in the district of Midnipur; he had to leave his ninth-grade studies after his mother passed away and he had to look after his father along with his older brother.

When he was born, a lack of adequate polio injections affected one of his legs, leaving him with a limp. However, hunger and the need for money made his father send him off to Delhi with his uncle to look for work. From there, he could help support his father, who does the seasonal work of knitting fishnets.

His destiny brought him to our door – and with him came the fragile issue of having a fifteen-year-old cripple. I still remember my mum being against the idea of getting work done by a cripple. The superstition was that a cripple brings bad luck; that's the India I cannot come to terms with. If only our ancestors were more aligned with sense, then they would've invested in more noble thoughts. But then again, we had people like Swami Vivekananda and, of course, the British Raj.

I was glad he stayed. If he'd gone to another home, he would've definitely had a job – but would he be called a son?

He is not our domestic help; we all look to him as our younger brother. I remember when the ceremony of Rakhi was upon us, my sister and I would always tie a Rakhi thread or put *tikka* paste on his forehead. We would always run to his aid to help him when he would slip while bringing a glass of water. He would fall along with the glass but he would always rise up with dignity and with a smile on his face. That is his spirit.

Today, he is an accomplished man in his village; he has savings in his bank and looks after his father. He built a pukka house in his village, but the floods of 2007 in West Bengal washed away his hard work. My mum and dad stood by him – and why wouldn't they? Khokhon called them Maa and Baba.

I was sitting with a cup of tea in the big veranda, watching Khokhon feed grains to the flock of birds that gather every morning. There was always water kept aside for them, so they could quench their parched throats. In our house in Delhi, no one went away without water or sweets; it was my Maa's order, as she reckoned any person who walked through that door was God-sent. After all, we're all God's handmade creation and so are the birds.

The birdsong made me feel as if they were talking to each other, wishing each other good morning in their own language. The birds made me realise I was in search of my own language, my own identity.

Just then, I saw a parrot, caught between the window grills. It was fiercely trying to free itself, wanting to fly for salvation, and I wanted to fly with it.

Somehow, the parrot set itself free. I was jealous of its freedom. I felt trapped when it flew away; it got so far away that it left just a tiny impression of a dot on the vast skies of Delhi.

The day went slowly and the jetlag eased; finally, I was feeling at ease with myself, and then I was hungry. But first, I needed the internet connection. Maa and Baba never felt the necessity to have an internet connection; to them it was like an unnecessary expense when they could talk on the phone.

I missed everyone and everything about Melbourne. To have internet connection felt to be not only my birthright, but my only window of escape.

To have a wireless broadband in Delhi was not only unique, but it worked quite differently. I was not only out of touch with the world here, but also not an expert guru on technology. I turned to Khokhon to arrange for my key to the world.

In this chaos of arranging internet and fitting in with a life I wasn't used to anymore, for the first time in twenty-four hours, I felt happy. I was about to share the twenty-first century with the people of Delhi.

Our flat was among the bungalows of rich businessmen and well-known cricketers of Delhi – to me, it meant nothing but to some, it meant everything. I never belonged to this house, not only because it didn't 'belong' to us, but I had no childhood memories to fall back on.

In India, the telephone lines are not underground and invisible. Here, the lines are on rooftops and sometimes can cross over the electric poles, so one can mistake them for electric lines.

I was actually more amazed by this unified chaos than ever before. It still works today as it did eleven years ago.

So, in less than twenty-four hours, I not had heard the gossip of my neighbourhood, the fiasco of having an internet connection that stuck a cord with me. It just reminded me how I missed being a part of this chaos.

The recommendation was obviously to have wireless internet and to lock it. What more did I need? I had a man come to the house with the CD to install it – and what a service! I didn't have to move a bone to hunt for it.

I was quite amazed to see Khokhon's expression and even more fascinated when Maa would join in this gossip. They conversed with such zest and with such force, I just wanted to keep hearing the gossip over and over again.

Just opposite to our bungalow, was this beautiful bungalow in white; from our veranda I could see its marble floors. Outside, stood a range of cars belonging to that house – I guess each member of the family had one car for their luxury, and a driver to go with it! Oh well! That is the trend nowadays in Delhi.

Next, I heard about a so-called wealthy woman from another bungalow, who left her husband so that she could be with her driver. She was in her early thirties. I happened to see her that very afternoon, while she was out on her afternoon walk. Of course, it was none other than my Maa who pointed her out to me.

I said to Maa it was a nice hobby she'd adopted over the years. To that Maa replied that she wasn't the one who was so inquisitive of others' business, it was the *kaamwalis* (maidservants) who kept their ears and eyes open when they went from one house to the next to work.

In one way, I was amused that like every other woman in India, she knew what was happening around her – but I was also sad because she wasn't like other women who would be interested in gossip. Her children were all overseas and Baba was always busy, so now she had more time, I think, with Khokhon and the *kaamwalis*.

It still happens in India, that people are attracted to imported gifts – 'Made in USA', or in my case, Australia. It doesn't matter which part of the world it came from, as long as it's *not* made in India.

 # BABLI

> "For we women are not only the deities of the household fire, but the flame of the soul itself."
>
> **Tagore**

I was on my balcony, wiping away tears when I looked up to the sky. Dark clouds were brewing; suddenly, I heard a big roar. At first, I thought it was a thunderstorm and then I saw a massive bolt of lightning; I felt the building and the concrete floor of my veranda shake. I thought we'd been hit by an earthquake, but then something in the sky caught my eye.

A big ball of fire was fast approaching. I looked around – the streets were empty, not a soul, as if the entire neighbourhood was deserted. I looked up again and the big ball of fire had nothing to do with nature's fury – I had just witnessed a flight crash.

I ran to take refuge behind a concrete wall that separated the main house from the veranda, but my legs wouldn't budge; my entire body was numb. The tail of the airplane fast approached. I closed my eyes; I wanted to scream for help but I couldn't. Then there was this massive sound.

After a few moments, there was absolute silence. I slowly opened my eyes and saw heavy smoke. I couldn't see any bodies, and there was absolutely nothing else, just fire and smoke. I still couldn't speak but I managed some courage to walk towards the wreck. I saw the tail of the flight – 'Qantas'.

I closed my eyes in fear and refused to open them again, feeling the calmness it brought to me. I had to see more – I couldn't just leave my eyes closed. I opened my eyes. Maa was still snoring beside me, the house intact and the clock in the living room still going. Tick! Tock! Thankfully, my misery ended with the realisation that it was a bad dream.

The next morning, I didn't say anything about my dream. I was still trying to make sense of it all. Maybe I missed Melbourne and subconsciously it came along in my dreams – or perhaps, it was just a silly dream. I tried to shake those feelings out and concentrate on the moment.

At the breakfast table, I felt pampered; Maa was cooking delicious paratha stuffed with cauliflower. The smell was irresistible and made me hungry, only lifting my spirits. Each bite of the delicious, oily bread was amazing.

My laptop was working and I wanted to write an email to Isabelle, but I ended up writing the first chapter of my book. Time flew and my appetite for food grew.

I decided to eat everything today, from samosa (fried dumpling stuffed with potatoes and peas) to *aloo chaat* (potatoes covered with mint, chilli and tamarind chutney) to *bhel puri* (puffed rice mix with hot chutney) and *aloo tikki* (potatoes and chickpea batter with a blend of spices). It was a gastronomic avalanche and I was quite ready to indulge.

I asked Jethu to be my partner in crime and gave him my never-ending list of carbohydrates galore when he went for the next round of groceries to the market. I was hesitant to step out of the house. I presumed the best thing for me to do would be to eat. This was all so wrong yet so good, but I thought this could be a breakthrough, a way to reintroduce myself to my roots – through my stomach!

The assault was imminent; my stomach felt the merciless pain but I'd missed these amazing savouries. I was deep into my gastronomic affair to the point of no return.

I took a good spoonful of *aloo tikki*, another spoonful of *bhel puri* and two pieces of samosa in my mouth, not a care in the world. I covered them with mint and tamarind chutney. Maa looked at me with surprise when I helped myself again to *aloo chaat*. 'Eat responsibly,' she said. I was in Heaven until there wasn't a single tiny piece left on the plates.

No one was there to share with me, nor did I have the courtesy to ask anyone – I was the ultimate case of gluttony.

***

It was half past one in the morning when I woke up with a sudden pain in my stomach.

I twigged and turned; I felt it could've been menstrual pain and thought to myself it would subside eventually. I waited for it to go away but then there it was again, and my stomach made a sudden gurgling noise. I could feel it coming, the glucose and the lactose all combined into one formation, desperately trying to find a way out – in my case, it was my rear side.

Trying not to wake up the entire house, I tried tiptoeing but the force was too much and I ran towards the bathroom.

I was quite conscious of the noise, but how could anyone ignore the unprecedented intensity of nature's call? I whispered, 'Bite me!'

I went back to bed thinking I was quite lucky to have narrowly escaped severe indigestion, but then my stomach proved me wrong. The pain this time was unbearable, as if I'd been ruthlessly serrated with a knife; the images of samosa and *aloo tikki* made me feel nauseous.

I ran towards the bathroom again and these attacks continued throughout the remainder of the night. Finally, I slept.

***

I woke up to the sound of Maa's morning prayers and to the cramp in my abdomen. It was far from over and now I realised what Maa meant by telling me to eat responsibly.

Baba came to check on me and his hand on my forehead was both soothing and consoling. 'Should have been more careful about the food you eat from outside, you're not used to it. No one knows what oil they use and for how long they've been using the same oil repeatedly,' Baba whispered.

Maa joined into the conversation and said aloud, 'Ten times, I recall you going to the bathroom.'

I laughed at her exaggeration but she could be right – I hadn't been counting. I was surprised that she was awake throughout the night to witness my ordeal. 'It's just indigestion, I'll be okay,' I said with conviction.

I soon realised it wasn't okay. It was a combination of dysentery and vomit – everyone was told about my little debacle.

Everyone living in our bungalow came to visit me, from the maids to the owner of our house. I made quite a headline. Soon, I knew the story of my indigestion would not only be the talk of the neighbourhood, but would also make headlines around the town.

I made a few visits to the doctor and received a daily dose of antibiotics, and of course, a formal warning to ease up with the deadly concoction of oily food and eating outside. I made an agreement to eat home-cooked meals moving forward.

After days of eating *khichdi* (a combination of rice and pulses), I felt stronger. *Khichdi* is supposedly good for people suffering with gastro.

***

After a few days, I decided to start the day with something different: a plain cup of tea and toast. Reading the newspaper, I began to feel my own struggle of understanding India again; it was a very strange feeling. I felt like India, though not as ancient – my history stood at the gap between the modern and the ancient.

To me, it seemed India was struggling to keep up with new-age values, a shift in culture and morality. Who am I to judge that? Every section of the newspaper was filled with the latest brand names and the latest cars advertised.

To me, the staggering divide between the rich and poor was still astounding. But there is some good news too; the culture is not in total disarray. Thank God to the mothers who still wait for their sons to come home, so the family can enjoy a decent dinner – where the dinner table is not a spread of Subway or Pizza Hut but the common man's roti-dhal and *sabzi*. Where there is still one sport that dominates the nation: cricket! Mother India is still at its best.

I soon realised that I was among the patrons of Cricket World Cup fever.

Suddenly, another section of the newspaper caught my eye. In the north-east of the country is the state of Mizoram, which is unique in its culture and beauty. The entire land is covered with lush forest and mountains. But what caught my eye in the newspaper was a baffling story. Today, Mizoram made headlines for the world's largest family: thirty-nine wives, ninety-four children and thirty-three grandchildren. I was shocked at this. I wondered if it had anything to do with love. Probably not!

That night in my room, I pondered, the TV in the lounge room interfering with my thoughts. I was about to prove myself wrong, that love does not exist – it's only a metaphor for sex – just when I heard Baba calling my name.

I went into the lounge room; Baba was enjoying his favourite Indian whisky. I sat next to Maa on the opposite sofa.

We talked about Melbourne and our lives when the topic took a certain turn: my brother. My parents felt that he abandoned us; in a way it is true, he indeed abandoned his family by closing himself off from us – but it was his choice. He still has a door open in his bloodline, where hatred conquers love and where blood is always thicker than water.

Baba was talking about his struggles during the 60s in Kolkatta, so that we could have a good life. In those days, business was tough, but he did it to raise a family. He ran away from Bangladesh because my grandfather married again after my grandmother's death. This tore him inside and so he left everything to make it on his own. Later he was joined by my great-grandmother – and I was fortunate enough to see her, although the only connection that I could relate to was my father's.

He'd told this story many times, but to me it sounded new each time; he told it with such enthusiasm. After all, they're his memories – and the only thing one can relate to is who they are, where they belong – it's their *asthitva*, their identity. For him they are his memoirs.

I asked about the meeting of Maa and Baba. He'd told me this innumerable times as well, but today I wanted to hear it again. My parents had an arranged marriage and though Baba is eleven years senior to Maa, they have an amazing mutual understanding. When Baba came to see Maa, she was thirteen and he was twenty-three; he was forced by my great-grandmother to see Maa. She was made to wrap a sari on top of her pinafore, and she had short hair and was skinny like a stick.

Baba immediately said no, as he had no intention of getting married to a child – but in those days, it was common to get married early.

Maa was asked to walk so that my great-grandmother could see if her walk was 'auspicious'; she did indeed pass the test and married Baba. The marriage didn't take place until she turned sixteen, as she was a child – but in saying that, it was still true that when Maa got married she was a young girl, who was taught by Baba how to cook and how to drape a sari. Maa and Baba still fight over this, as he would say that he taught her how to drape a sari and she would say she already knew how.

The tale, however, took a sudden twist today with something I'd never heard from Baba – and it was the reason I changed my perception about love from a few moments ago. 'I have a little secret to tell. Before I met your Maa, I was somewhat in love … what they call love at first sight.' Baba said that in his slight tipsiness, taking a sip from his glass, smiling away while looking at Maa.

I was thrilled to hear Baba's well-kept secret but also because it was his love story, from before he met my mother, and I was intrigued to understand his grasp on love.

It happened in 1967, two years before Baba got married. He used to go to Ashutosh College, the Shyama Prasad night school, every evening after his work as a clerk. This was Baba's struggle period.

I think it's better to narrate his story in his own words.

'I used to take the same tram to the college and she would be sitting in the corner of the back end of the tram. Our eyes would often meet, but you see, we never spoke; we just looked at each other. And then one day, there she was sitting in the front row of the tram.'

Those days in Kolkata, the trams were old; I was visualising Melbourne's old trams that still run free for tourists through the city circle, but my thoughts were interrupted by Baba.

'She had her bag or handkerchief opposite to where she was sitting so that no one could take the empty place. I don't quite remember what it was, handkerchief or bag, but what difference does it make?'

For a brief moment I was looking at Maa: she was smiling quietly. I turned to Baba. 'So, what happened next? Did you ask?' I was mindful of asking, as it was his secret and I didn't want to embarrass or argue any point that was fundamentally incorrect to him. It takes a lot for a parent to share their love story with their child.

Baba took another sip of his whisky. 'Unfortunately, nothing happened. We were speaking with our eyes and had lot of questions at this point … for example, a name to start with. The tram came to a halt and she suddenly stood up, smiled and walked off. That was it, I never saw her again … not the next day, or the day after or forever. That was it for my short love story.' He took a deep breath and had another sip.

'Why didn't you walk behind her or make the first move to ask her name at least?' I hesitated to ask more; I respected his love story.

Baba began, 'There are some things best not said, just felt. Silence speaks a million words.'

'Why didn't you follow her? Maybe she wanted you to make the first move?'

He looked at me straight in the eyes and said, pointing at Maa, 'I say thank you to her. If I had followed her that day, I wouldn't know what love was – and neither would I have had these forty- two years of blissful married life. And I wouldn't have you, would I? Love is felt and it has an endless space in the heart, my *shona* (dearest).'

That night, I thought about the entire evening. To me, love was still undefined – I was more confused than ever. To feel love: is it to stay silent forever, or to experience the feeling one has to wait forty-two years for, to say that they had been in love and lived to tell the tale of meeting a stranger in a tram? Perhaps it is that then: to feel love in that first look. I now know where I get that 'love at first sight' from – but the difference between Baba and me is I say it aloud. I don't keep it growing in silence.

The next morning, I was still consumed with the thought that love isn't about keeping silent and was tormented by Baba's love story. However, I was looking forward to meet Babli.

Babli was Maa's masseur; she was the only one in the family who was the breadwinner, as her husband was without work these days due to a motorcycle accident. She was married to a man from Nepal; she eloped with him when she was sixteen and they'd been one blissful couple ever since.

She had to let go of her family, as they didn't approve of the marriage. I wondered, why is love such a tenuous task? Why did people have to leave others so that they could be with their love? It was mind-boggling for me to comprehend – to lose and to gain.

Maa's sciatica pain was Babli's gain – needless to say, that's how they met through common acquaintance.

I brought some gifts for Babli and her two sons as Maa requested, so two Tim-Tam packets and a bag written with 'I love Melbourne' later, she finally smiled.

Babli is shorter than me and has long hair tied as a braid. Her chubby cheeks and short legs were somewhat like mine, but her smile and laughter were wonderful.

She was grateful for the gifts and later she was talking about Australia: how she wanted to go there one day for a holiday. Each and every consonant, verb and adjective from her mouth was like a firecracker. To me, she spoke faster than light and was loud like no one else, with spontaneous witty charm.

'Come here Didi (sister), let me see your skin and what massage can I do for you,' Babli said to me. Though she's one year younger to me, she still addressed me as an older sister – it's very common to call everyone 'Aunty' and 'Didi' in India.

I said to her I would do a *malish* (massage) and all the beauty essentials, but not for free – she had to take some money. I guess I must have offended Babli, as she didn't look a happy chappie.

Later on, I found out from Maa that she hardly takes money from her and, as I'd now bonded with her as family, she couldn't take any cash from me either.

In India, it is very easy to form relationships as a 'relative'; you can refer to your friend's mother as your mother.

I should've known better, and if I had lived in that world, I would've sustained the same capacity – but that was not me. I'm my own person and my world is different, even though Maa and Baba don't agree with me. Perhaps I'm ignorant.

Babli was doing Maa's massages and I sat quietly next to her, watching Babli's solid hands move around Maa's calves. They were in their normal rounds of neighbourhood gossip. I was convinced that they both shared a peculiar bond.

Babli went on, 'You know Didi, Mrs Mehta introduced me to your maa, when I saw your maa it reminded me of my mother and that's the reason no matter how busy I am, I will still come to her aid and do massages for free. It's not charity; I called her my mother, so I have to honour that.'

I smiled and asked her, 'So tell me how you got married at sixteen.'

She covered her face with her *dupatta* (scarf). I must have embarrassed her.

She slowly began, 'Didi, I ran away with my Nepali, he used to stay opposite to where I used to live. Every day he used to see me when I played with the kids in my shorts. I didn't know what love meant then, but I used to like him. He used to tell me that "one day you will elope with me", and I did when I was seventeen. Sometimes I think, why did I elope? And now I have to look after everything: the house, the kids, my family and his family.'

I looked at her and realised that marriage is indeed a chore. Why do people get married to suffocate?

My thoughts were cut short and Babli was smiling, massaging Maa's ankle now, then she said, 'Whatever I say, Didi, that's beside the point, but when I go home after a hard day of work, he always cooks the rice and the dhal for me. To share a meal with him and the children is a blessing.'

I laughed aloud and both Maa and Babli looked at me in surprise. I guess they both expected me to say something very touchy, but instead I thought about a joke that a neighbour once told me: the true meaning of 'husband', is that the wife laughingly beats the crap out of her husband, like the drums in a music band. The joke is actually very funny in Hindi: from 'husband', *hus* in Hindi means to laugh and 'band' as a music band. I couldn't help it and burst into a roll of laughter.

'What happened?' Maa asked and Babli looked at me puzzled. So before making anything more complicated, I shared the joke and I thought they'd take it pretty badly, but to my surprise I had a full house of giggles.

On that note, Babli looked at me and said, 'Well Didi, it's your turn now. Come, let me do your Brazilian!'

I knew this was Babli's sweet revenge. I just smiled.

# THE FESTIVAL OF COLOUR

> "Perhaphs I will become a ray of sunshine to be embraced by your colours. I will paint myself on your canvas."
>
> **Amrita Pritam**

*F*or my Western friends, the festival plays out when Hollika was burnt. In Hinduism, a devotee of Lord Vishnu called Prahalad was about to be burnt by the evil king's sister, Hollika. Being the King's son, he refused to worship the king and would only worship Lord Vishnu. Hollika was granted with a God's wish that she could never be destroyed with anything. Her evil ways were only to honour her brother and whoever got in her way; she would destroy them without haste. So Hollika decided to burn Prahalad alive.

She laid Prahalad in her lap to burn him alive, as she knew he would be burnt and she is immortalised by the wish granted by God himself.

Someone once said that the colour of life is the colour of people around us, and I think that's true in every sense. Around me were pink, yellow and green faces: little children playing with water pistols and throwing water balloons to every passer-by on a rickshaw or even a pedestrian. 'Oy! You wretched mongrels, Holi is not until next month, you little devils – come down and show your faces or I'm coming up!' After many swear words, there would be silence until the next victim.

In this chaos I had to come back to reality; we were looking for a place to rent, as Baba was fed up with Maa's complaints of the house. Well! We had our own big house in Kolkata but due to Baba's business problems, it was still under litigation between himself, the tenants and the bank.

He left his business empire in the capable hands of a few good men, but such is greed that even the trusted become the most unfaithful. He continued on his journey to promote his films and wanted his company to go public – and that's when everything fell apart.

This happened twenty-five years ago, but the effect still showed in our lives. Baba always expressed his deepest anguish to Maa that he couldn't provide a roof over her head. Their love was unique; she always smiled and expressed to him that he conquered her with love, and that's more than a rooftop. When back into reality, she would complain of the pest-infected kitchen – and then love would conquer everything again.

However, saying that, Maa and Baba got quite emotional when they spoke about their lives in Kolkata. I was little, so I remember very few things about Kolkata, my hostel days and moving into Delhi, but I can contemplate what they've been through. If there was any disagreement between us, or if the thought of my brother would bring them down to tears, Baba would often cry and say, 'You were all little when we left the Ballygunge house, holding your hands and coming out of it with nothing ... no jewellery and no clothes, just three pairs of little hands.' I would often feel sad but not until now did I actually understand his pain.

He built that house in the heat of summer; Maa, while heavily pregnant with my sister, her first child, supported Baba from strength to strength in supervision of that house. In every part of the house there were memories: in the corner of the kitchen, in the living room where he had parties and where all the well-known figures of the arts and cinema raised their toasts in honour of Baba, in the veranda where he would drink his first morning cup of Darjeeling tea. I would be at Maa's dressing table, trying her makeup. It's where my childhood began with my siblings, only to end on foreign shores.

Perhaps if I was there today, I could fall back to those brick walls, taking shelter under them and cajoling them to make me fall asleep. Perhaps there I would begin to find myself again.

He lost that house to litigation but kept the hope of building another house, which he achieved after sixteen years. He built that house to keep his dreams alive, but we were so caught up in chasing our own dreams that we never had time for his. We lost that house too; not only that, there was chaos in Delhi in 2005, caused by the Indian government demolishing houses that were unauthorised or had unauthorised floors. The new houses couldn't have more than three floors. Our apartment was built in 2003 and it still came under that law, as it was on the fifth floor.

The builders milked money and the policeman milked money – but Baba and Maa didn't lose the house because of that. They lost that house because we couldn't keep up with the promise of sending money in time for his monthly instalments. His hope was crushed in one go – and he was the only person, I guess in the history of mankind, who went and submitted the keys to the court. In years to come, the entire building would be knocked down.

In 2005, I left everything in Melbourne to be with them again. Perhaps it wasn't because of my parents, but because I wanted to escape from my own failed marriage. I wanted to write about this sooner but I had no courage until now. The beautiful colours of Holi around me perhaps gave me the courage that I need to pen this.

I lost a lot of friends after my divorce and I felt vulnerable with my new friends. I eventually disclosed my divorce to my new friends, realising it was time for me to let go of my past. Perhaps this was the way of re-introducing myself to my friends. People will judge, no matter what one does.

Thomas, an Anglo-Indian from India, was the best thing that happened to me during my early days of Melbourne – that's what I thought at the time. I married him; he was a lot older than me, but at that point everything seemed right.

He had abundant love for me and together we built a business and a home. I fought with everyone just to be with him; even my parents had to accept him for my sake. It was hard for them, very hard. Baba didn't speak to me properly for three good years, but I always called him, and from Khokhon I always heard how he was doing. My brother was living with us at that time but soon headed off on his own ways.

I was lonely when I came to Melbourne, and with it came the enormous pressure of business; with no friends and family, I was drawn into my own shell. My siblings had their own dreams to follow. I never quarreled with life; I let it play its own sombre tunes to me, until one day I realised I had to make a choice.

Did I marry Thomas because I wanted a father figure in my life? Did I miss having an important person who could dictate my life? I loved my father very much, but most of my childhood had been spent without him. He had been travelling the world for his movies. After his business problems, he left us in a hostel to deal with the situation in Kolkata alongside Maa.

Did I have a normal childhood? Perhaps I did, perhaps I didn't. I would be waiting in the hostel with my sister when everyone came to visit, and then suddenly we'd be alone when no one came.

Perhaps those images haunted me when I found solace in Thomas' friendship and I thought that the best thing for me was to accept his invitation to his friendship. Loneliness can sometimes make us do more than we bargained for.

We fought the world to prove our love for each other; at the time, it felt right. He used to call me *memsahib*, meaning madam. I was his *memsahib* for five years, until one day I woke up knowing that I didn't want to be married to him anymore. No arguments, just nothing. I was asked to close the business – and yes, it was a joint decision; no one forced me into that. I did it because I wanted to have a life. However, saying that, I was becoming the person he wanted me to become. Does marriage do that to you? I was thinking day and night but I wasn't ready to become the other person yet.

I started a job because we needed the money to pay bills; all our money had been invested in the business. We were happy in crisis but when marriage becomes a chore, it becomes lifeless, boring and without feelings. No matter how much you love someone, it becomes suffocation – and that's what happened to me.

I needed a bond, a common ground ... perhaps an understanding. For me, love was feelings! It does come with test and trial, but what was the point of me being tested over and over again?

I secluded myself from everyone to be with the man I loved, only to realise the thing that I wanted the most was the thing

I needed to be away from. Maybe I mistook his kindness and friendship for love. Did I date any men before him? No!

He always told me to accept the way I am, and I always sincerely accepted him the way he was. Unfortunately, he never accepted me for who I was. I was scorned at for marrying a 'sugar daddy' but that didn't bother me – I just wanted to be with him.

He took good care of me, as a husband would do for his wife and a friend would do for his friend, but then I opted out of the marriage because there was no common ground between us anymore.

If I went out to a party or with a friend, he would be happy for me, but when I returned he'd be quiet, drinking himself silly. I would be made to feel guilty and later he would be ashamed. Love cannot be shameful or guilty; it should be soulful with sanity.

I was young then and I didn't know what was happening, but I knew I wasn't happy in the marriage. It took me another six years to realise this. The only thing that was common between the two of us was the business. To me it meant everything, like a child to his mother – and when a mother loses its child, she blames everyone and everything.

That happened to me: a part of me got lost with the business and I lost Thomas forever. We could have talked things out but I didn't want to, and to some extent neither did he, as things would've been the same by the next day.

When the time came to look after him, I abandoned him. When my parents lost their house, I found the easiest way to take refuge – or, one can say, an excuse to protect myself.

I penned down this history of mine to seek redemption from Thomas. I looked outside to the massive Delhi sky; the sun was setting and I felt an enormous peace within. It took six long years to forgive myself whenever I thought about Thomas. I could only think about his love and send a silent prayer of forgiveness across to him.

I was in touch with him when I came back from India for the first time in 2006, after our divorce was finalised. I didn't fight for anything, nor did I ask for anything. However, he did ask me to take over all the business debts. I thought I owed that much to him and I did it as my repentance, as my forgiveness.

We bonded rather well. He helped me rebuild my life, and he did everything possible to see me settle. I think the distance between us made us feel that we're better together as good friends – it should have always been this way. Then, everything changed again.

Everything made sense to me when I told him I was leaving again for India. He didn't understand or want to know why – he just blamed me. He blamed me for leaving a job and a life behind that he thought he was helping me rebuild. Thomas said something harsh to me: 'Forget the money you owe me, that I helped you with when you came back to Melbourne – you're on your own now.'

I never asked for his help; it was his choice to help me. It was his participation in putting my life together. I could've said no, but I didn't.

It struck me then: I was once again living someone else's life. I understand that his anger was justified; he was my friend and he wanted the best for me. At that point I felt my anger towards him because I was angry at myself for letting everything go wrong in my life, and whenever anyone said things I didn't want to hear, I blamed them. I was indeed reading too much into things.

That was the last time I spoke to Thomas, losing myself, yet again, in the equation of forgiveness. Was I enjoying being the victim?

If he didn't want to speak to me, then I respected it and I hoped that one day he would. I knew we would talk again.

I wiped a tear from my eyes and whispered, 'Forgive me Thomas as I'm trying to forgive myself for hurting you.'

'Where are you?' Baba called my name. 'Come here, let's get ready – we need to go and look at this house, it's just across the road.' My thoughts interrupted by Baba.

I slowly wiped my tears and went to get my slippers.

***

We reached our destination and were greeted by two hustlers – I call them hustlers, but really they were brokers. In Delhi, real estate is a booming business thanks to the influx of people from interstate and neighbouring countries for jobs. Even tourists these days rent flats to be with the locals; big offices and hotels also top their list. The hustlers or brokers (whatever you call them) are either yours or the landlord's; they just need your money.

The flat was in a house basement, but we entered from the back of the house as the keys to the front were missing. The flat had an inspirational feel to the 70s art deco, with tiles all over the place.

Maa was carefully looking at the flat, trying to get as much detail as she could about the flat while Baba discussed the money side of things with the broker. I liked it because of the neighbourhood, not because of the house; to me it still wasn't where I could belong and serenade my aloofness. It was indeed very compact.

Maa was concerned about where she would put her temple and the broker jumped into the scene. 'Here!' He was pointing at the main entrance of the hall, where there was some kind of a partition to the main lounge.

Maa's temple is like having another family within a family. All the gods and goddesses had a home within, complete with clothes, utensils, bath essentials – and the Holy Scriptures, from where Maa would recite her morning and evening prayers.

In Hinduism, you take care of your gods like you would take care of yourself, and I thank my maa for passing it on to us, as it was passed to her by her elders. Our gods and goddesses not only have two meals, but a siesta included too. Each hour has a meaning; when to pray and not to pray is crucial. *Shayan*, meaning to rest the god to sleep, is important, as is waking the gods up in the morning and for the evening prayers.

The bathing of the deities is important too: everything needs to be clean and their perfumed water – which is especially made for the deities' bath – cannot be put into the common drain. The water is collected separately and put into plants.

Maa also has winter woollies for the deities in winter. Beautiful jewelled frocks for Radha-Krishna in the summer and gold garlands for Guru jee and Goddess Durga make her temple come to life.

My Maa's temple speaks to us. When you enter our house, you are already touched by its spirituality. God lives in every one of us.

The next few weeks went with packing. Packing was strenuous; from one cupboard to another, the clothes went into the hands of Maa and me, and then straight to Khokhon. He tucked them away neatly into the suitcases.

The same thing happened with the crockery; Khokhon took it from the showcase and the kitchen cupboards, passed it on to me to wrap, then I'd pass it to Jethu to neatly put away in the cardboard cartons.

Maa's temple was taking most of the time. It was made of marble and wrapped in bubble wrap and fabrics. She was careful as during the move to this flat, the movers forgot to pay attention and therefore broke the foot of the marble temple.

It took five men to move her temple, and ten people (including us) to shift the entire flat. Finally, we moved. First, the temple went in and then the rest of the house; it was already established where to put the temple (the location the broker mentioned earlier). The temple had to be south-east facing and, where the sun rises from the east, her *tulsi* (basil) tree was kept outside adjacent to the position of the temple; Maa would water her every morning, also lighting incense sticks and a *divaa* (similar to an oil lamp).

It took one week for us to settle in. Maa's first request was the temple and then the kitchen; the rest of the flat fell into place. Babli visited with some *idli* and then the next day with *papdi chaat* which made those lazy days special.

We were just beginning to settle in when the shadow of doubt regarding this flat began to creep into Maa's mind. The question of moving arose – I felt nervous again.

The flat had no balcony (naturally, it was a basement) and so my connection to the outside world narrowed down to my laptop and phone. Through emails and phones, I was speaking to Issy and my sister. My sister and I exchanged life via Skype and it was a fantastic opportunity for my parents to see their grandchildren again.

I still felt insecure about myself; it felt as if there was nothing to look forward to anymore. I lied to my sister and my friends back in Melbourne that I was having the time of my life and my routine consisted of nothing. My waistline was running in all directions; I ate whatever I could find.

***

One day, Babli came over and I asked her again if she knew anyone who had a yoga centre, or some kind of gym where I could at least make myself useful again. I remember her mentioning once that she knew someone here in this neighbourhood, running a class or gym of some kind. Perhaps this could be my avenue. After pestering Babli, I finally got Poonam's number.

The chat with Poonam was brief; she mentioned her centre's philosophy was to keep the bodies of Indian woman in mind, and she had lots of cardio sessions and yoga. She mentioned her fees and I decided to take her offer and see her program for myself.

I was still uncomfortable walking alone. I didn't know why – perhaps because of the forever-gazing eyes of people, continuously judging you. Maybe because of the strange stares one got from the men around; they seemed to mentally undress every girl walking past them.

I asked Baba to drop me at Poonam's place; I very carefully noted her address, as my sense of direction can sometimes be quite frightening.

The room was tiny with false wooden flooring. I was shocked to see a jam-packed room with twelve different women cramped in. The women varied in shapes and sizes, but they all pumped in full force to the pop songs of the 90s. The majority of women were in their mid-twenties. I seriously didn't think I would fit in but I wanted to give it a go.

'Hi! I'm Nandita.' I extended my hand to Poonam. She just smiled. I gave a brief rundown of who I was. I presumed Poonam would be a woman in her mid-twenties but she turned out to be in her early fifties. Fit as a fiddle.

She was slightly taller than me with a body to die for, a perfect silhouette. Her grey hair was a sign of her age, but she didn't do anything with it to manipulate her age; in fact, she was showing it off like a vintage wine.

I liked her instantly. She was timid at first but I always make it comfortable for the other person in a conversation so that things become easy and natural between us.

I gave a brief introduction: I was here from Melbourne for a holiday and I was writing a book. She was intrigued and mentioned that her daughter settled in London, while her son was completing his doctorate at Harvard.

'I don't know why this generation does this? It's good to study abroad but then one needs to give back to their country too. What do you think? Where do you see yourself living, here or there?' she asked me bluntly. Before I could answer, she interrupted. 'You know, my son says, for whom do we do anything in this country? Here, no one is appreciated. I always wanted him to work free for the poor, and asked him to join a government hospital, but sadly, today nothing is for free, everything is commercialised.' She made a very sad, animated face.

I think my smile must have given it away; she looked at me, disappointed at first, then she smiled too.

I said to myself I could maybe, just maybe fit into this scene. I was judged by what I wore and they were shy – a formal hello would've been a difficult venture to get into – but somehow, I felt this could be my escape from being alone.

I told Poonam the session was good – I lied. I was bored but my muscles were in pain. I chose to return, but to the morning classes, strictly at seven.

***

Back in Delhi now. The next few days, I felt like my life had been cultivated into another routine. I was glad that it was Friday already – no more mundane aerobics routines. Sometimes, it's hard to keep up with just staying fit. This was the life that I gave up before returning to India, and I was being trapped in going back to it, even if it was purely my choice.

My parents' anniversary was coming up and so was Holi. They always made it a point to go to our guruji at his ashram, in Vrindavan. I was excited about that; I'd waited for the journey since I landed in Delhi.

We woke up at four in the morning as usual, to fill up water, but the air was filled with enthusiasm for Vrindhavan.

Vrindhavan was two hundred kilometres away, taking us into another state of India, Uttar Pradesh. If we had leaped another hundred kilometres, we would've been in Agra, the land of the Taj Mahal, but we were not going to see the Taj – perhaps another day.

The sun was at its peak and Baba tired from the huge trucks driving past and the huge traffic jam on the Delhi-Uttar Pradesh border. Finally, the saga ended. Traffic rules have no meaning here whatsoever; whoever is in charge of the car has to be on guard! Overtaking cars on Indian roads meant careful manipulation.

After a few halts for morning tea, we finally reached Vrindhavan. The roads to Vrindhavan felt as if the gates of Heaven were opening for me; on every wall of a house or a building was written, 'Radhe! Radhe!' (the Vrindhavan name for Radha). There was a sense of calm even to read the words in my mind.

Radhe! Lord Krishna's beloved – lots of us mistake her for Lord Krishna's wife, but they were never married; she forever remained his consort. Their symbolic love story became a testament to Hindu religion; thus, the worship of Lord Krishna is never fulfilled without Radhe!

***

Holi was just around the corner, so one could spot colours on the walls. It is believed, the true essence of the festival of Holi originated from Vrindhavan. Here, Lord Krishna and Radhe, along with his herds (which were known as gopis) shone in the colour of love.

It is believed, and I heard this from Maa, if you pass a cow on the road and if it doesn't move, just whisper in its ear, 'Radhe! Radhe!' It will move and give you way.

Vrindhavan is a magical land, a spiritual guide to those who have lost their way. The small town is famous for its old, ancient lanes, where the houses dwell closely attached to each other. Some of the houses are medieval and one can see the cracks on the walls, perhaps able to tell their tale of history in time. The progress of India still shows here with cars and buildings, but I guess this is the only town in India where the old will never change for the new.

Seeing the old buildings, still the same as when I had last been here, left a soothing effect on my soul. The billboard showed that plots for homes were available at less than fifty thousand dollars; Maa would read it and say to me, 'One day, I will have my retirement home here with God.'

When you enter Vrindhavan, there is a temple built by ISKCON, founded by Swami Prabhupada. The swami had gathered undivided followers from all around the world, giving Hinduism a new meaning to the West.

Culture is slowly dimmed by greed and want. It is true, though, that too much God and too little life can leave you wandering in between – but sometimes it is good to be lost in that life. Perhaps I was feeling insecure from this sense of being in a lost and found game.

It is also known that when the ISKCON temple was built, there was an uprising, as many of the Hindu pundits in Vrindhavan opposed it. The westerners from ISKCON were considered outcasts, but true devotion overcomes obscurity and it has been proven love conquers all; the love for Lord Krishna has won over the wrath of a few sacred Brahmins. Religion has no face or colour; worship begins with the mind and God seeks those who seek God, without discrimination – only faith. Lord Krishna has given his faithful the right to be known as Brij Bashis, meaning the dwellers of Vrindhavan, but sadly, the temple is still referred to as the 'temple of *gores*' meaning the 'temple of whites', and even today the whites are still not allowed inside the temple of Banke Bihari (another name given to Lord Krishna).

We entered the narrow lanes of Banke Bihari and into the commotion of the town, amongst the flower vendors and the little shops selling *ghagra cholis* and little sparkling dresses for Lord Krishna, to the lassi (sweet curd drink) man with extra *malai* (crème on top).

We had to lock the car where we parked, just a block from the lassi man, as there were monkeys in the area. The monkeys would run away with glasses and we had to be careful while walking with eyewear. If an offering was not made to them (fruits of some kind), it would make them angry and they would run off with their stolen items. Stealing was minimal here; the most common form of stealing could possibly be pickpocketing. We were once like the monkeys, and they've now accrued this habit from us. How unique!

The lanes of Banke Bihari were as narrow as the other lanes of Vrindhavan. But this lane was special. When you entered the lane on the left, there were little shops selling flowers and sweets; on the right, there were shops selling deity frocks and shops for paintings and souvenirs. A few shops later on the left, there stood the medieval temple of Banke Bihari.

To enter the temple, we had to climb a few flights of stairs. Maa was still haggling with the flower man, who was selling her a big garland of *mogra* (jasmine) and raised flowers.

The huge crowd to see Lord Krishna was overwhelming and I felt as if I was summoned here by Lord Krishna, to witness it all. The chant goes somewhat like this: 'Radhe! Radhe! Shyam mila de!' Meaning, 'We're requesting you, Radha, please help us meet with Shyam (another name for Lord Krishna).' To seek Lord Krishna, one has to go through Radha, his lifelong companion. The gates of the temple where Lord Krishna or Bihariji dwelled would close – then the chant would begin again and the gates would open for the *darshan* (sighting).

We circled the temple and when I was face to face with Bihariji, I couldn't pray for anything – I was too enchanted with his gleaming, diamond eyes. I wanted to pray and say something but I was almost lost in that dazzle; all I managed to say in a whisper was, 'Forgive me.' I folded my hands to kneel but the line was enormous and I was pushed away. For a moment, I couldn't see Maa or Baba, and we were scattered among the ocean of people who formed waves to seek Bihariji.

Finally, I saw Baba speaking to the pundit and I quickly ran towards him. Maa was a few steps from them, lighting incense sticks. I was listening to the chant of the priest, who prayed for me in Sanskrit and then put a *tikka* of sandalwood (paste of sandalwood, only applied through fingers) as a *bindi* on my forehead, along with a garland.

Maa joined us and asked the priest to give me blessings and pray for me. I thought to myself, no one's prayers are of any help to me – only if Bihariji sought me himself could I be redeemed.

Maa was telling me the different types of *puja* (prayers) offered to Lord Krishna: one with flowers and the others I don't remember.

Radha was never married to Lord Krishna but she is worshipped alongside him. We all make requests for his *darshan* through her, but a woman living with a man before marriage is still considered shameful – or, for instance, having an affair in a marriage. She becomes the gossip of neighbours, just like the woman in our neighbourhood who lives with her driver. It is only forgiven if you're rich or famous – nothing for the mediocre. In saying that, things are changing, but I believe it will take another few decades to change the mind of the people. People who can accept their gods and their lovers in any form and shape can surely accept lovers in any forms.

I felt guilty for such thoughts; I came here to pray and seek something to see and feel. It needs no religion to argue that it is a sin to have an affair while married, but what about the people falling out of love, having a change of heart and realising they fell in love with the wrong person, followed the wrong dreams and aspirations? The list is endless.

I felt terrible and I tried to pull myself out of such negativity. This time, I concentrated on giving alms to the needy sitting outside the temple. Such was the poverty here: Lord Krishna wears diamonds in his eyes and the old have to beg for two rupees. I was perturbed and felt like giving everything, yet all I had was a bruised soul – but if someone had asked for it today, I would have given it anyway. If someone could be made happy with my bruised soul, then why not? Take it all!

I felt I was also a beggar, coming all this way to beg for redemption and forgiveness, but no one was offering me that today; everyone was giving food, money, but could someone give this poor soul a drop of forgiveness? I will bathe in it for years to come.

I felt nothing. The gates of Heaven were slowly closing on me. I felt conceited and ashamed.

I couldn't explain it to Maa, who was happy with her spiritual enlightenment. Perhaps I would try my best to be happy for her.

As she was giving alms, Maa was looking for someone in the crowd. 'Who are you looking for, Maa?'

Maa looked at me, puzzled. 'There is this old Bengali woman who would always be here, you remember, who reminded Baba of his grandmother?'

When I came here a few years ago, and before that too, there was this old Bengali lady who would beg for alms. Upon receiving, she would bless Baba a lot – and so every year they would visit Vrindhavan, with or without us. Baba once bought her a lassi drink – and with that, he invited upon himself the entire flock of people seeking alms. Baba is Baba; so great is his heart that he had bought lassi for everyone.

'Maa, maybe she's not here today – perhaps she's gone somewhere else.'

Maa nodded to my response. 'Yes, perhaps you're right.'

The trip to the ashram was beautiful; it was getting hotter, no doubt, but my soul was still burning for the rush of God to consume me all over. We were crossing over to the other side of the Yamuna River and we were forced to put the windows up due to the dust. From my window, I could see the dust rising up from the riverbanks, leaving behind a trail that fogged the entire road behind. I felt like standing there and letting the dust consume me so that I could go and bathe in the Yamuna, which, like the Ganges, has the power to wash away sins. I felt a teardrop at this thought and I thought this would be my act of contrition.

I walked slowly behind Maa and Baba to hail the boat that would take us to the other side of the riverbank. I could see the white roof of the ashram. I overheard Baba saying to Maa that during the monsoons, the river would swell so much that this road would be closed and all the cars diverted to take the long route. The long route could only be done by circling Vrindhavan.

I noticed on our way to the ashram that a barefooted man with a *dhoti* (cotton cloth wrapped around the waist) was circling the river Yamuna and had a rosary in his hand, maybe that of *tulsi* beads that Maa and all the women of ISKCON would chant with. I silently prayed – I couldn't remember to whom the prayer was offered but I said, 'I wish all goes well in my life and if I find happiness in my life, then I would circle the entire Vrindhavan, just like that, without any give or any take.'

We reached the ashram banks; the serenity of the ashram was slowly taking over my fatigue. I couldn't feel anymore, as if I was in a trance.

Our guru jee, Shri Devraha Baba, has many disciples around the world and is often known to the West as the Nanga Baba, the 'Naked Guru'. He would have only a loincloth wrapped around his waist and would sit in his *maachan* (a makeshift hut made out of clay mud and hay).

He always chose his disciples carefully from the swarming people who came to visit him. He would call them near to his *machaan* and with his left leg, he would bless the disciple and offer him some *batasha* (sugar-coated tablets).

This is known as *deeksha* by a guru. My parents were blessed with *deeksha* in 1982. We sat before the *machaan* – the mud and clay floors underneath, a relief from the heat outside.

After the *samadhi* (union with the divine) of Devraha Baba in 1994, his two disciples took responsibility for the ashram. They were young when I used to come here as a child; now they have become 'Older King' and 'Younger King'! ('King' is not always associated with statehood; it is also used for a yogi or maharishi, meaning a saint.)

The ashram was peaceful and quiet and I decided to stay here for a while, but then Maa wouldn't leave me alone.

Some believe that Devraha Baba was the *maharishi*, who travelled all the way from the Himalayas and then back. The first generation of Nepal kings witnessed his presence and so did the era of Gandhi. But according to Maa, he himself is Lord Vishnu, who has come to redeem people. I just know him as my guru jee and all I know is he summoned me here today to talk to him without any fears.

Miracles of God happen in small dozes and so do *guru kripa* (Blessings of the Guru). My journey with Guru jee had already started when I was eight; I had to wait another twenty-six years to come here to seek some kind of answer. He is always with me, walking besides me and talking to me – but even though I 'understood' this, it sometimes wouldn't make sense. If he is there, then why is there so much misery in my life? If he walks beside me, then why so much fear? If he talks to me, why can't I hear him more clearly?

I needed clarity – and when that internet scandal engulfed my life a few months ago in Melbourne, I realised I had lost all faith in my life, and a part of that was my belief in miracles and God.

Sitting under the *maachan*, I was more lost than ever before; maybe I still wasn't letting go of the fear and numbness in my heart. I believe in Devraha Baba. I've seen him in real life and heard his voice, but I've never witnessed his miracle. I needed his miracle bestowed upon me so that this broken and bruised soul could be transformed. I prayed and hoped my tears wouldn't betray me here, in front of my parents. I wasn't ashamed to cry in front of Guru jee, but my tears would break my parents and I wasn't ready for them to be a part of my sorrows.

We went to the Shiva Temple and with water, milk and honey we bathed the Shiva *Ling* and Guru jee. It was suddenly very funny. While lighting the incense sticks, watching the *shiv ling* being worshipped, it occurred to me that I had in fact worshipped the *ling* many times, but today I felt like asking the one question that was burning inside me all these years. After all, it is the day of contrition.

Ling means 'a part' in Sanskrit and the Shiva *ling* is the groin of Lord Shiva. Daily, millions of Hindu women pray to the Shiva *ling*, including my mother and sometimes me, by pouring water on the ling. It is believed that to pour water on Shiva *ling* calms the soul of the men in our lives, but such is the plight of men these days that no water or prayers could calm them. Then again, if you believe in it, there's everything – and when you don't, there's nothing.

I just smiled at my thought.

Finally, the pundit did his honours by wrapping a red thread around each of our wrists.

The ashram was empty so I walked around the gardens; there I began to say my prayers again.

Our guru jees were ready to meet us. He referred to my Maa as Mata jee (Hindi word for mother) and Baba as Bhagat jee, meaning devotee. As women are never allowed to touch the feet of all rishis and guru jees, we just offered our prayers and sought blessings from a distance. Other people joined in too.

Chote Maharaj jee began his *pravachan*, meaning holy mass, and I was all ears to his sublime words. He said, 'It is very difficult to control the mind, but one who can control the mind is a winner.' I had goose bumps – was he reading my mind already or was he judging me? But he is one of God's disciples – he cannot judge me. He was reading my mind indeed.

He was talking with his hands now. 'If your mind wants to pray and believe as you want, then the mind will pray and accept what you believe – it will come out naturally. If we try hard to put our mind in practice, it will never occur to control the mind – it has to come naturally.'

I remembered the muffin talk with my shrink a few months ago – today it all made sense.

He kept speaking, but I was lost in the entire topic of mind and control. If only I knew how to control my mind, I could've controlled my life too, and this wouldn't have happened – I wouldn't have been lost. Secretly, I prayed to Guru jee while circling his temple. It was on the left-hand side of the entrance. I climbed up the stairs and I saw the entire Yamuna River; at the same time, someone rang the big bells that hung on the ceiling of the temple.

It is believed that if you pray and someone rang those temple bells, what one wishes for could become true. It was a superstition but I still hoped.

I wished I could stay for a longer period of time, just to listen. I wanted to stay here until Guru jee's *yogini* (chanting). After lunch at the ashram, we rested in the gardens for a while before heading towards Delhi.

While going back on the boat towards our car, I was in some kind of a trance, or perhaps the events of the day left a profound feeling in my soul. I gathered that provoking my own thoughts not only led to my own confusion, but also to my own destruction. Let things happen – we cannot change them, but what we can change is the course that we take, and that truly comes with the mind.

I saw the sunrise while going towards Vrindhavan and now I saw the sun set while going back to Delhi – after darkness there is light and vice versa, just like in the quest for change.

***

I woke up the next day feeling calm and happy, trying to control my mind. What would I do now? Perhaps, I'd start with staying happy. My parents' 42nd anniversary was in two days. I wanted to show them that I was happy; in recent days they hadn't felt that happiness at all from me, so it was a perfect opportunity to show them, I'm here and I'm happy.

Black forest was Maa's favourite cake, and pineapple, Baba's favourite. Half and half, it was that simple!

I ordered forty-two red roses in secret from the flower man who came daily to bring in flowers for Maa's temple; of course, my partner in crime was Khokhon.

I thought about the food – what would they like? Maa doesn't eat meat, so it had to be a combination of chicken and veggies.

I confided in Maa when Baba went for his afternoon nap. 'Maa, is it possible to have a small dinner party for your anniversary? You don't have to do anything. I will arrange it all.'

Maa seemed unhappy with my proposition; she looked annoyed with me. 'What's the use?' I knew deep down she quite liked the idea but, childlike, she wanted to be stubborn. I laid down the plan in front of her: some pappardelle and meatballs (and soya balls for her), Italian salad and mocktails for drinks. It would be a blast, I promised. After much persuasion and pestering, I got a yes! We pestered Baba together, and then it was a plan!

The next day I woke up happy and calm. It had been a long time since I felt like this, after leaving Melbourne and arriving in Delhi with all the worries in the world. Today it would be different.

We were all getting ready to go to INA Market in South Delhi, when the television was flooded with news of the tsunami hitting the pacific coast of Japan; the vision was too much to bear. I remembered what happened with the floods in Queensland, a few months prior, but this was far worse. Even a country as vast as Japan couldn't escape nature's fury.

In one of the visuals in the news, a woman was waving a white scarf or a cloth. She was standing on what looked like a balcony that was once her house, now half-immersed in water. Such is the hope of survival that even in the worst of disasters, one gets the courage to toughen up. Where was my courage? I wondered for a long time until my thoughts were interrupted by Baba.

Once in INA Market I was flabbergasted with the amount of Western produce that I would always buy in Melbourne. I'd come here before but I'd never had any of that produce in my shopping trolley, or the knowledge that I would have today. How strange was that? I felt like I was walking in one of the markets in Melbourne and it was saying to me, 'The world is just a market away.'

I remembered the parrots in the old house, how food united them. It felt appropriate to think that food also unites countries, people and religions. In a way, I was uniting my parents' anniversary with love – and love of Italian food.

INA Market was Delhi's answer to Coles or Woolworths for Australians. All the diplomats would come here to shop and due to the vast influx of tourists and expats, it was booming. It must have always been like this, but today I saw it with a new pair of eyes.

From gnocchi to endives, you name it and you got it. So, I ticked off my shopping list, from pappardelle pasta to sun-dried tomatoes to balsamic vinegar.

I was careful with the money I had; to begin with, I had little, as out of three thousand dollars I gave some to my parents. It would have to last me for the months I stayed here. After that, I didn't know what would happen. It didn't matter today because I was happy and I found my Melbourne in this little INA market.

Baba and I went to the wholesale flower market in Connaught Place after my morning routine and I bought two dozen Oriental lilies and roses. People were buzzing everywhere, as this was a wholesale market. This market was open from five until ten-thirty every morning except Monday.

I was easily spotted as a tourist to everyone with my short hair and blond streaks, and it was a pity; at every shop I visited, they would speak to me in English and I would reply in Hindi. I was a bit nervous as I didn't want any attention. The price haggling was always there and I was amazed to see some of the tourists had learned this trick too. I wondered if they did it in their own country. I was happy to pay the price they asked because they were selling flowers, the sweet scent of nature and love.

***

The kneading of the mince chicken started and the pounding of fresh oregano consumed the entire kitchen. Roma tomatoes were all diced and chopped carefully for the sauce. I bought hot Nando's sauce, which I was surprised to see being sold, just in case for the spicy tongues. I was following all the basic requirements in Issy's recipe; I had to do justice to her, after all, as it was her pride and everyone in my family would be feasting on it.

Maa was beautifully draped in her mauve cotton sari, which had golden dots all over. I forced her to wear her pearl necklace and her beautiful brown lipstick – for me, with or without lipstick, she would forever remain my beautiful Maa.

Baba looked like a smashing Bengali bridegroom in his silk kurta and pyjamas. It looked as if I was here to witness their union just like it was forty-two years ago; only their facial and physical appearance has changed, and they now had a thirty-five-year-old daughter next to them.

Maa was nagging Baba to wear another kurta, which infuriated him and he spoke to Maa quite rudely. 'Does he always speak to you like that?' I asked.

Maa her head lowered for a split second in shame to hide her tears. 'Yes! Sometimes he does when he gets too puzzled with business.'

'That's no excuse! Men!' I showered her with my own annoyance and then I thought for a moment – it's their time, they both need to be happy. I spoke to Baba and conveyed my deepest request. 'Come on now, the two of you need to make up, don't let a kurta come between the two of you.'

He sat in one corner of the room and Maa on the other. I felt as if I was amid two naughty children, scolding them for playing pranks on each other. I felt like their mother; to some extent I had to do something, so that these two naughty kids could make up before the guests arrive. Thankfully, they did.

I was preparing the mocktails to pour in the glasses. Maa couldn't keep up with the shape of the balls; they had no eggs in them to bind them together so they turned into mince, as if they were eating pasta bolognaise. There were vegetarians too, so I cooked extra vegetarian pasta and soya balls.

Everyone enjoyed the garlic bread as an entrée, but when it came to the main course, I was watching with anxiety and trepidation.

The verdict was mediocre. They didn't find the bland taste too much to their liking; Baba had to add some more salt and chilli to spice it up. Typical Indian, I thought. But Maa enjoyed it and I was filled with gratitude to be able to share this with them. I took a glance around the room: they all were happy and yes, they did commend the chef, but that moment was priceless.

I was happy and I raised a toast to Issy! They were all confused but it didn't matter anymore. I was feeling tipsy with joy.

They cut the cake and as always, it was eggless cake from their bakery; like all the other times, they wouldn't stop raving about it. Seeing Maa and Baba happy was worth it. My gift to them was this moment of laughter I could share with them – and with it, they gave me a gift too: to be their daughter.

***

The next day, I packed some of the meatballs and pasta for Poonam. After all, my audience was only Maa, Khokhon and Jethu. It just occurred to me; maybe it could be a good way to make new friends.

I was getting pretty bored, and with boredom came snacking. I ate everything that I found in the kitchen. It was ridiculous but I gave it no thought; I let my mind control me again. I forgot about Maharaj jee's words when it came to all the special Indian sweets for Maa's temple; these sweets were given as *bhog*, meaning they were offered as God's lunch and dinner. After all, God would be just as hungry and tired as us.

One of the sweets was *gujiya*: flour dough deep-fried in ghee, dipped in rose syrup and saffron, and stuffed with sweetened dried fruits. They were insanely delicious and in abundance during Holi. They came in all different colours, shapes and sizes; I liked them so much that I had an entire kilo of those little devils disguised as *gujiyas*. Each bite reminded me of the fairy tale of the leprechauns and the wasted wishes. Today, that leprechaun was granted a fat wish.

The next day Baba went and bought, to my guess, the entire *mithai bhandhar* (sweet shop): from *kaju burfis* (cashew nut pastry sweets) to *kaju* rolls, *rasmalai*, more *gujiyas* and my favourite, *gulab jamun*. The entire recipe for getting diabetes in one day – no wonder India is the world's number two country for diabetes! Moving forward, I decided not to let loose a greedy tongue, as I didn't know what it might wish for next.

The day before Holi, we were gearing up to go to the New Delhi Kali Bari temple to offer our prayers and hear 'Satya Narayan Katha', meaning the real words of Lord Vishnu! Kali is one of the most popular Hindu goddesses, often known as the goddess of destruction (which is not her only role). She exhumes the soul from ego, and thus transforms the human soul in the cycle of life.

The Kali Bari Temple was looked after by the Bengali pundits, famous for Durga Puja and one of the temples that were close to the hearts of all Bengalis.

I was walking up the flight of stairs along with Maa and Baba when I came face to face with Goddess Kali. She stood in her room (the temple) just as I last saw her two years ago. She was shining, with a gold and crystal chandelier hanging on the ceiling over her room. Festival lights and big copper plates laden with fruits lay on the floor to be offered to her in prayer. Standing immaculately in her red sari, she stood while resting one leg on the chest of Lord Shiva, one of her hands holding the head of the Demon King Mahishasur.

It is said that when Maa Durga (or the goddess Durga) went to destroy evil and the demon king Mahishasur, she was unstoppable and she had to transform herself into this form of anger, taking the face of Kali. No one could stop her ferocious ways and so it happened that all the gods came to Lord Shiva, who was her husband, to make a request.

The only way the wrath of Kali could be stopped was by forcing oneself to the feet of Kali; Lord Shiva had to throw himself at her feet to calm her down and make her realise that the path of destruction could have almost destroyed her love.

Sooner or later, we need to calm ourselves from destruction. I don't have a man to do that for me; in fact, all the men who came into my life destroyed me. Perhaps I needed a real man who could calm the path of destruction in my heart.

At this thought, I looked at Kali again; it was as if she was sticking her tongue out to me, mocking my thoughts and telling me it takes another class to be in the league of such men.

***

The Next few days were mundane. I didn't want to go outside because I was scared that I wouldn't be able to enjoy Holi with the same enthusiasm I did years ago.

After the morning rituals, seeking blessings from the elders and God by applying *gulal* on their faces and feet, I wished them all Happy Holi until another year. I retired to my room and took my laptop out to send the email to Issy that I had written to her after Maa and Baba's anniversary.

Before sending the email, I read again how I blatantly lied that this was exactly what I wanted to do: come here to India. I was ashamed that I had to write about being so happy to be here. I was forcing myself to be happy in Vrindhavan, in the ashram and planning my parents' anniversary. So, to get through with the guilt of *not* being happy, I decided to add more to the email, about Holi.

THE MISSING PEACE

> "Many men cry Peace! Peace! But they refuse to do the things that make for peace."
>
> —Martin Luther King Jr.

Folding clothes one by one with Maa, I felt helplessness sink in again. It felt to me as if, with each towel I was folding, I was packing away every bit of anxiety and loneliness. I needed to breathe again. I wanted to go out, perhaps learn something new. How many books are there to read? How many movies are there to see and people to talk to? How much can I write every day? I felt unnerved by the whole idea.

I thought the miracles of God were slowly fading away. I said to myself, 'I have to divert my mind.' I thought of calling Sandy and so I did. She was happy that things with her newfound love were going very well; she filled me in with her life and work in Melbourne. 'So how is India, are you happy?' Sandy asked me suddenly.

The response came slowly. 'I'm very happy and made new friends but I don't see myself living here forever – of course I'm coming back.' I lied to my friend I was happy, but what I said about going back to Melbourne was true.

The next morning, I went to the aerobics class, although I wasn't sure what I was doing there; the girls were at their best, trying to impress each other. I thought I needed a change from the 90s music and the aerobics. I asked Poonam, 'When is the yoga class starting again?'

She looked at me strangely and said, 'Do you want to join? Hmmm … okay, I'll speak to the yoga instructor, but tell me, are you not enjoying here?'

I thought of telling her the truth, but sometimes, reality bites. I felt withdrawn from the entire conversation so I decided to tell a little white lie. 'Oh no Poonam, it's actually that I have to start getting into shape and I want to do two hours every morning – one hour with you and one hour of yoga.' I felt sick at this idea but I didn't want to upset her.

Poonam introduced me to the yoga instructor: 'This is Nandita; she wanted to join your yoga classes. Just explain your timings and fees and when she can join.' Poonam then left for her second morning class.

The yoga instructor was shorter than me, but her knowledge about yoga was commendable; she knew all the moves and was explaining them to me with roaring enthusiasm. I got well and truly into the conversation and lost sense of time.

When I returned home, the energy of two hours of exercise was driving me nuts; with that, I thought I deserved a big lunch and I ate everything once again.

***

The next morning was easy. I woke up at six-thirty in the morning, brushed my teeth and waited for Baba to drive me to Poonam's.

Once there in the room, I was quite baffled at what I saw. It was an empty bedroom and the floor was covered with four rubber mats. She asked me to be barefoot, so I removed my socks and slowly made my way onto the mat. 'What the hell am I doing here?' I was continuously saying to myself. The instructor began with the Surya Namaskar (salute to the sun); my body went into spasms. The instructor was explaining the importance of this move: each morning when the sun is just on the horizon, the early morning light is essential for endurance of the body. It helps us with breathing capacity.

For me it was too painful to keep up; my body was not flexible at all for this move.

Slowly, the four mats were occupied by women who didn't smile. I thought it was either too early in the morning for them, or the diamonds in their fingers made them too classy to smile.

The next technique was a breathing technique – Anulom Vilom Pranayama. One has to breathe in from one nostril and breathe out from the other. She was telling me it is good for people with heart disease and depression. I needed that in abundance, I thought, to help keep me in line.

After all the techniques were shown, we were all asked to close our ears with our index fingers and say *om*! 'The echo of this word helps our *kundalini* rising and helps us stay happy. "Om" is the sign of peace and tranquillity – and within that, the entire world roams around.' The instructor was explaining it to me, detailing the importance of peace in our lives, and it was amusing to me because I've known this word since I knew to read. Never once had I actually put this into practice and when I did, it was remarkable; the word 'om' touched every part of my body. It was telling me that I had been lost indeed.

I nodded a big yes to the instructor and expressed my deepest gratitude.

The grilling started when the session with Poonam began. Beside the point of how the yoga class went, I was quizzed if I would continue; as always, my answer was yes! Next to us was Astha, who was standing and listening to our conversation. 'You're going to do yoga and aerobics too? Wow! I used to do yoga in the evening, but due to my exams I cut it short these days. If Yoga aunty sees me I'll have to run for the door.' We both chuckled at this idea.

Astha was a normal twenty-year-old whose passion was travelling to Europe on summer holidays with her family and driving her Honda around the city. She had a sweet tooth, a cricketer as her boyfriend and a fixation with the world ending in 2012. Anyone could mistake her as a European with her fair skin and bubbly chatterbox personality. We clicked instantly.

'Come on girls, move your legs up – stop chatting there, you two!' Poonam was asking us to shut up and get on with the class. My legs were up in the air and my bum was on the floor – it just didn't take off. I whispered to Astha, 'Damn, my bum is getting too old for this fiasco. How do you manage to do that beside eating and drinking all those chocolate shakes?'

Astha giggled. 'I've known Poonam aunty since I was ten years old and have been coming here since I hit my teens. I used to go to school and cry, but one day she took charge of my tears and since then the bond's been inseparable. So many girls you see here would always be consulting with her or their mothers with aunty. She just knows what to do.'

The class finally ended. Poonam and Astha were heading to Astha's car when Astha asked me to join them, as she lived just a block from me. We were talking about life in general when we reached Poonam's house. She said, 'You know, we always live the dreams of others – when we're young it's about our parents, but we say that we're carefree and there are no restrictions. When you're married, you have to let go of all your dreams. I had so many ambitions in life and when I had children, everything was lost, meaning my ambition.

'I cannot live without my children. I was born to be their mother and then you realise their dreams are yours ... and you try to keep happy. I was a tomboy once but now if I make any gestures, like if I put my hand on a man's shoulders, I will be given the moral lectures – but that's what our society is, very closed. I cannot do kitty parties because that's what the other women would do to kill time. I have this centre to kill my time. Men have their business – I have my women.'

We all laughed and decided we should have a party to celebrate our being gutsy. I didn't know why she said that and when she got out of the car, but I saw a reflection of myself somewhere in her words.

I looked at her house and then visualised her – maybe that house was too big for her emotions and she needed an escape. Sometimes money isn't enough to buy happiness.

Yoga and the two-hour session weren't until next week, so I had to use the time to participate in the aerobics session. The next morning, I decided to walk alone to Poonam's. I remembered the conversation from the previous day about how she was a tomboy and still is one; if she could walk the streets of Delhi with her shorts on, so could I with my spandex.

The area I lived in was known for stray dogs. The municipal corporation did its work when it wanted to, especially when they got a complaint from one of the nearby rich mansions. Then, they would come with their trucks to accomplish their mission.

Some would say the dogs would be put to sleep – others said they were put in corporation homes.

It's still a mystery to me how they're handled. India didn't have an official association or body preventing animal cruelty, nor could I imagine an agenda or forum on the horizon; concern for a mere stray dog is farfetched. Politics, greed and power are the plight of people, rather than thinking about a dog's habitat.

The stray dogs are as plentiful as the common man, sometimes roaming around the vegetable vendors, screening through for cheap deals. When one can hear the howling and barking after midnight, one can assume it's their nightly meeting to acknowledge which meal was best provided by which house, or which lanes had the best leftovers to offer.

The *chowkidars* (guards) patrolled the neighbourhood and they lashed the streets of the neighbourhood with their handmade wooden sticks. The stick was more of a tough rod that helped them to screen for any robbery in the area – and, of course, to keep these dogs away. These were old habits passed on to the new generations, but somehow the *chowkidars* maintained their duties of safeguarding the suburbs of Delhi.

Unfortunately, we turn a blind eye to what matters the most – the stray dogs. Roads were expanded, new mansions built every day and the city illuminated with lights, but the suburbs, the city's dogs and the common man are all overshadowed within this glimmer.

I was walking to Poonam's and nearby there was a construction site: a new mansion being built. To get to the other side of the road, I had to cross a temple, a school, a park and this construction site. Outside the construction site, I saw a few men getting on with their morning routine, brushing their teeth and making tea. What I saw next was appalling: two stray dogs on top of each other, mating. The men were rather amused with this spectacle.

I was caught between these men and the mating dogs, and I was wearing spandex – it didn't help. I ran!

Poonam was alone when I reached her, and I overheard her speaking to someone on the mobile. She smiled at me and I smiled back. 'It's my mum. We are talking about her sister, who's not well,' Poonam told me. No matter how old you are or how young, the bond between a mother and a daughter is inseparable. She reminded me of my own Maa, when I would call her from Melbourne and she would do a zillion things in between talking to me, while fishing for news of my brother.

I was front in line at the class, facing the mirror. I took a good look at myself and the face had no familiarity today. I looked like a person trying desperately to fit into the lives of these women. I was trying so hard, I forgot that someone else's costume wouldn't make me look any prettier or more unattractive – it would still be me.

Jerrean, a beautiful Malyalli from Kerela, was a Christian mother of two and married to a Hindu; she nudged me so hard that I had to come back to reality. We all called her Jerry. She's funny with an outspoken character. This was a result of her profession in hospitality; you had to be brave and smart to choose this profession in India. We would often crack jokes about each other and the moves that Poonam would have us endure.

We were doing push-ups and I surprised her by saying, 'Ten more of these push-ups and you'll forget all the positions of Kama Sutra.' Jerry laughed at this. The jokes would go on and on until the end of the class.

I learned later that Jerry would sometimes fill in for Poonam, which perfectly suited Poonam as she had to take care of her two sons; the youngest one was just eighteen months and the older one just joined school. Her husband was a manager in a five-star hotel and due to the nature of his work, they would travel from one city to another, each time transforming their lifestyle. My life was somewhat like hers, with the only difference between me and her being that she was happy.

***

Maa and Baba were planning a trip to Jaipur to see Bala jee, Lord Hanuman. He is the mighty monkey deity, the most popular among the Hindu believers. He is worshipped for his strength and agility. He worshipped Lord Rama and when he and Sita went into exile, Hanuman went with them.

Lord Shiva assured safety of Hanuman with a band (a Holy Kovach) that would protect him for life. Lord Hanuman is popularly known as the monkey god in the West and is very popular among the bachelors in India. Lord Hanuman never married and his powerful scripture is read by thousands of bachelors every morning, known as the Hanuman Chalisa. It frees men from evil and from fear.

According to Hindu belief, there are four Yugas or ages, meaning four ages of life. Satya yug was the age of truth and morality. Dwapur Yug was the age where the human race witnessed violence and imbalance. This period ultimately led to Kalyug. Tetra yug witnessed the change of people's emotions, where human beings are not bound by any form of task or mission. Kalyug meaning the age of deception and vice.

Each age had an Avatar to save us and so will this age. According to Maa, for a very short period in Kalyug there will be a few glimpses of the 'honesty' of Satya yug, where peace will prevail. Perhaps the birth of the Avatar was in my life. I'm yet to be transformed in my own version that I want myself to vanish and disappear from this darkness.

We were all ready by five in the morning, as we had booked a car. The drive to Jaipur to see Bala jee was five hours and we had to make it back to Delhi safely, before the trucks dominated the highway.

I was wearing a *salwar kameez* (long top and tight pants with a stole) I bought when Maa took me out shopping before going to Vrindhavan. Maa requested I buy this, as it would make her happy and it's always nice to be a part of the culture at the holy places. In a way, I was ashamed. I had discarded the things I was born with when I made my life in Melbourne, but karma somehow gets back to settle scores.

The first stop was to Bangla Sahib Gurdwara. Baba is also an avid follower of the Sikh religion and this Gurdwara (Sikh house of worship) is the biggest place of worship for all Sikhs in Delhi. This Gurdwara was built after their eighth Guru, Guru Harkishan.

Every religion is welcomed in their Gurdwara and no one is rich or poor. The Gurdwara has no deities – just a holy book known as the Guru Granth Sahib, which is wrapped in silk. The holy songs of devotions (*kirtans*) are sang in praises. It bears a huge resemblance to the golden temple of Punjab but there is no difference in the devotion and service, since Sikhs believe the biggest devotion is to serve people, the human race.

The setting of dawn and the *kirtans* at Gurdwara was magical, like a scene from an old classical film. The city was still half-asleep, not witnessing the spectacle. The stream of light made its way through darkness, slowly waking every creature in the city to remind them another day has arrived. The busy streets of Connaught Place were empty, but for the flower market opposite, it was business as usual. I was somewhere else; that moment seemed so surreal, as if I was captured in a movie reel, reliving someone else's life.

The highway to Jaipur was a long stretch and this highway was quite different to the one from Delhi to Uttar Pradesh that we took for Vrindhavan. We were travelling to Rajasthan, the north-western region of India. Once we left Delhi, we were on a road in between desert and vegetation. The trucks were overloaded with people and at one point there was nothing except our car, the ravines of Rajasthan and the long stretch of roads. It was my first time visiting Bala jee, another avatar of Lord Hanuman and I was eager to introduce myself to him, to know him and understand his supreme powers.

The road to Rajasthan seemed new. I felt oriented towards this new connection but still harbouring doubts and fears. I thought I had depleted all my spiritualism since I'd returned from Vrindhavan, but in this fresh spiritual source could be a marvel of an idea, just an idea. It is difficult for anyone. I still had spiritual bandwidth to keep me going but I wanted to have it all, till I was full and had reached my ultimate potential, seeking truth.

After five hours, we reached the main gates of the Salasar, in Churu district near the city of Sikar. The gates read, 'Bala jee Salasar'. On both sides of the road were huts made of mud, and beneath were the sands of the desert. It didn't feel as if I was in 2011, I felt like I was lost in time. The cactus trees, the brick factories, the tractors, the bullock and camel carts, and the women with their oversized skirts and sticks in their hair still walking around. I suppose some things never change, especially in rural life. they've accepted the change but have found nothing special to celebrate.

The car came to a sudden halt in a busy marketplace with small stalls for flowers, sweets and souvenirs everywhere. On the left was a huge brass door and Maa signalled that to be the temple of Bala jee. We asked our driver to park the car and we went inside the temple. There were people everywhere – inside, it looked like a small town – and we left our shoes on the shoe rack before walking inside, heading to the courtyard.

A huge fire burned on the left-hand side and next to the fire were trees filled with coconuts tied with red cloth with golden lace or *chunni*. Maa was telling me that this fire was very holy and had been burning for 'thousands and thousands of years'. It was her exaggeration, but I was quite happy to write this part as 'thousands and thousands of years'. We waited for our pundit to arrive; everyone who is a regular to this temple should have a pundit.

We stood in line with hundreds of followers from all around the country. The line was slow, but then it moved and I was face to face with him. I just stood there, trying to sense his questions for me, but all I could do was marvel at his gold attire and the silver lining on the door of his temple. For a split second, I wasn't thinking like myself. Was I summoned to come here? I felt as if I was here before but was never physically here. I pointed a question directly at Bala jee. I was so in awe, and I felt I was contradicting God's presence; between such feelings and the other people showering him with divinity, it made me confused about offering my prayers.

Soon the line forced us outside the temple. I felt I must have angered him as I was being pushed outside. Maa always told me Bala jee summons his devotees to come – but was I a devotee yet?

Soon the pundit came with the sweets that Maa and Baba wanted to offer Bala jee, and we were once more inside the temple. Again, I was face to face with him. I closed my eyes and prayed with my hands folded: 'If I was not with you here, could

I envisage being anywhere else? Show me a way – where do I belong?'

Just at that moment, one of the pundits put a huge garland on my head. Was it a sign of him introducing himself to me, welcoming me?

Afterwards, we took a circuit of the temple from inside, with people and yogis reciting verses and tying the sacred thread. Finally, at the back of the courtyard we were asked to tie the coconut with the red cloth to the tree. No matter how hard I tried, it would slip right out, but with the help of Baba I was able to finally do it.

The coconut tied to the tree with *chunni* signifies the devotee's wishes. Every devotee prays for their wish to be fulfilled; it is believed that when it is, the coconut drops. One way or another, the devotee knows that their prayers have been heard.

I didn't wish for anything spectacular; all I said while tying the knot on the tree was to show me where I belong and I would give forty kilos of *gujiyas* in *bhog*.

We were now on the other side of the building, waiting for the lift to go up to the third floor to a centrally air conditioned lunchroom. There were some groups of men and women and each had garlands and ten kilos of gold around their necks. It must have been some big wish that had been fulfilled. However, the floor below us was this huge dining area where people were eating on large tables, one adjacent to the other. It is the common area; people who could afford pundits for their services got the air-conditioned lunch room.

Such is the state of money these days. Does God really want this? It's all our act of glory to show how much we care for our own comfort. I guess I was as guilty as the rest of them, waiting for the air-conditioned dining area.

Once we sat, the Rajasthani custom was to start any meal with sweets. I thought it was a marvellous idea; all the sweets I saw in the kitchen area were making me hungry. The huge *balushai* (Indian version of the doughnut: a flour pastry dipped in sugar syrup with dry fruits and deep-fried in ghee) was so delicious that I gulped three at a time and then also managed to have roti (Indian bread), paneer (Indian cottage cheese), and potato and pea curry.

There was a small uproar regarding some purees (Indian bread fried in ghee). They were the same group of people with gold laden all over them, who were waiting for the lifts with us downstairs. One of them screamed, 'We have given forty kilos of sweets and we demand purees!' I was astonished. In a place where rich, poor, fat, thin, ugly and beautiful doesn't matter, does it really matter to not have purees? They pray to thank God for their wishes being granted – why couldn't they be thankful for what they had? I guess that's the way we are. I continued to eat and prayed that they could have their purees so we could all have our peace with our food.

After lunch, we waited in the hall of the pundits, where one of them ran to get some *prasad* (food offering) from inside the temple. While we waited, I asked our pundit to narrate the birth of this temple. He was very excited to tell me but first he brought some cups of tea.

'It began sometime in 1811, when a farmer in the next village, while ploughing his fields, came across Bala jee's idol in his fields. Soon the word spread like fire in the village of Asota and neighbouring villages.

'That night, the king of Salasar dreamed of Bala jee. The king was summoned by Bala jee to get his idol to Salasar. The same night, a *thakur* (feudal lord) had a similar dream: Bala jee came into his dreams and summoned him to take his idol to

Salasar. When the *thakur* contacted the king of Salasar, both the king and the *thakur* were speechless. Hence, the miracle of 1811 stands today for all of us to believe that some way, somewhere, miracles takes place every day in our lives.'

Our pundit's eyes were shining like the saffron *tikka* on his forehead as he narrated the story.

It was time for us to go. As we left, we were chased by more alms seekers, who wanted to bless me with a happy marriage, children and a lot of money. I felt an overdose of blessings rushing my way.

What is wrong with people and their blessings? All I wanted from them was to take my money and bless me to be happy. I guess everyone's happiness here was marriage, children and money. They saw me as no different to them – and why not?

While leaving the Salasar Dham (Salasar pilgrimage site), I was recalling the story of how Bala jee was found. If miracles happen through dreams, was my air crash dream from a few months ago leading me to Melbourne? Was it my destiny?

I wanted to see a miracle happening too; I wanted my dream to envisage my possibilities. Would my whispers of prayers guide me to the right path?

Love, kindness and prayers are all forms of God. To love God is to love ourselves. But lots of us don't connect with this theory. I believe in what I hear, feel and sense – this day, I felt that Bala jee summoned me here, thousands of miles from Melbourne, to connect with him and believe in his miracles, as they happen.

A bus in front us, laden with people hanging out of its doors, came to a halt when our car crossed the bus. It bore an advertisement of a mobile phone: '*Yatri* on a journey'.

'Yatra' means a sacred journey to religious places for salvation and a *yatri* is the person who goes on this journey. I was indeed the *yatri* of this Yatra.

***

The next morning, I woke up from the car jerking. I was car-lagged after the twelve-hour drive to and from Rajasthan; I wanted to go back to sleep, but it was time to get up and do my daily ritual before going to Poonam's.

Next to our building, there was this empty plot where the caretaker lived with his family in a makeshift brick hut. They were getting on with their morning business of cooking and bathing. I tried not to disturb them and slowly walked out to the main lane. As the back door was used as the main exit and entrance, the empty plot next door was a shortcut to the back lane, leading to the main street. I took the usual shortcut, and through the back lane I crossed the temple and that embarrassing construction site. I carefully passed by all the stray dogs of the neighbourhood.

When I hit Poonam's street, I saw a black dog slowly following me; my heart was racing, and I tried to pace myself. I stood calmly in a corner, just to see if it stopped when I stopped. To my horror, it did, so I managed my dread and walked straight to Poonam's.

Once inside, I felt calm and relaxed. Poonam said, 'You look worried.'

I just smiled and said, 'Yeah, I suppose I'm okay. I think I was followed by a dog.'

Poonam looked at me and said with a laugh, 'At least by dogs and not by men. You are safe.'

I burst out laughing.

Just before the class started, the girl next to me smiled and handed me over the same wristband she was wearing, red, with 'Guru' written in Punjabi. I was truly touched and felt blessed. I just smiled and couldn't express my gratitude to her.

My ordeal with the stray dog was narrated with high drama by Poonam and everyone joined in the conversation. Jerry especially took a special interest in the episode and with her loud voice she said, 'What man? Haven't you been accosted like this before?'

I kept quiet and just chuckled.

I had company on my walk back home and was relieved. One of the ladies who usually started in the eight o'clock session was in this seven o'clock session and lived close to me. Kiran was a middle-aged housewife, looking to socialise and stay fit, after her husband left for work and her daughter went to school. We were getting acquainted with each other as we walked. 'So you are not married? Or you don't want to be married?' she asked. I wasn't ready to answer but she was waiting. This was quite personal, but I was in Delhi and here nothing was personal. If you say hello to someone or befriend someone just for a few moments of walking, then it doesn't matter how comfortable or uncomfortable you feel – it is their business.

'No, I don't quite feel the need to be married at the moment, or perhaps not …' I didn't say 'again', and I didn't feel the need to open a can of worms early in the morning.

'You should, you're thirty-five and it's always good to be in the honour of a man. Loneliness can be a dreadful thing when you grow old. You need a man to be loved.'

I nodded with a forced smile. She was right in some way, but how could I explain to her that men and I don't mix well? They always had the pleasure of hurting me.

Kiran continued, 'Aren't your parents looking for you? I should meet your parents and speak to them.' By now I was infuriated with this suggestion and getting very uncomfortable. I made the wrong choice to walk with her. Perhaps I should've controlled my fear somehow.

Sensing something wrong, Kiran managed to change the subject. 'You know, some of the stray dogs are mad here so be careful.' On the contrary, I was beginning to be scared more of the people here, than the dogs – at least the dogs didn't have a suggestive mind, they only attacked if provoked.

I bid my goodbye to her near the temple and walked towards home, only to be followed by the same black dog again. I wasn't frightened this time and I soon reached home, only to find Khokhon outside watering the plants. The black dog, still about two hundred metres from me, was wagging his tail. 'He's been following me since morning,' I said.

Khokhon just smiled. He asked me to follow him to the adjacent empty plot we used for the shortcut. It was empty and there was a cardboard box; Khokhon asked me to look inside. What I saw was unbelievable: inside there were four puppies, all asleep. There were two brown, one black and one stood out from the rest, white in colour. The mother of these puppies lay somewhere close by and I could hear the slow growling, commanding me to get out of there.

I took a step back and then I realised the black dog was still there, wagging his tail. He was introducing himself to me. For some reason he knew me. I smiled at being the chosen one.

I asked Khokhon to empty a flower pot; Baba joined me to help filling the pot with water and a steel bowl with milk. 'Baba, milk is not good for dogs,' I tried to advise, but his response was quite unique. 'It's an Indian dog, here everything is digested which is noble.' He had a point.

The black dog drank the water and the milk, only to disappear again. Soon he came back and behind him was the mother of those puppies. Baba poured some more milk and also brought out some biscuits from the kitchen pantry.

Why did they choose me? Was I similar to them, walking aimlessly in one direction, waiting to be shown kindness while no one felt the need to understand me?

I entered the house, leaving the dogs to drink and eat in peace, while the laundry man and a few neighbouring maids came to see the puppies.

In the lounge room, the Bengali news channel was in full swing. Jethu watched while peeling some potatoes. Many veterans from the film and art society of Kolkata were protesting against dogs and cats being buried alive. I couldn't exactly fathom what was going on, whom they were protesting against.

I sent a text to Sandy in Melbourne. 'I made new friends today! Four stray puppies and their mother. I was introduced to them by their father. They came and slept on the porch of the house, ate our biscuits and drank our milk.'

***

The next morning, there was senseless enthusiasm in the air. I was beginning to understand the mindless cricket fever in India – over the decades it has become bigger and better. I never grasped this game before but gave it my support because others in the house were fanatics. The World Cup was here in India and after a long time, I was again witnessing the fascinating and awkward madness of a nation.

If anyone wanted to see a united India, this was the perfect example: India on a cricket ground. No religion and no rich or poor, as if the gods of all religions were playing the game for them. All the newspapers were filled with signs like 'Go India' or photos of famous people regaling the Delhi social scene.

Cricket ignited passion in the yoga class too; it so happened that one of the girls was getting married to a cricketer in the following months, and everyone was curious if he was in the national team. One of the women – Friend was a designer and relatively well known for her work. Friend wanted to know whether the soon-to-be-married girl's wedding trousseau was taken care of, otherwise she would be very happy to extend her assistance.

The ritual of Surya Namaskar started, and I knew my body wasn't reacting to it anymore. 'These acrobatic movements give you the will to perform better in bed.' I said. They all burst out laughing and I wondered why. Perhaps I didn't phrase it properly. I forgot to add 'for a good night's sleep in bed'.

After a rundown of where I was from, Jerry asked me the inevitable. 'So, are you single, married or entangled?'

What's wrong with people here, how about 'what do you do'? Why do they always have to attach someone with somebody? 'No,' I said politely.

Friend, much to my surprise, invited me to do the rounds of the club scene with her; it didn't take me long to understand that she was a regular. She was telling me that once, in her own words, 'Out of all days, the day I choose to get drunk, my driver decides to get drunk too!' They'd argued as to who would drive the car. I just smiled.

Then she quickly returned to me being single. 'Don't you feel like being with someone? Thirty-five is young but you should have someone for your needs.' I knew where the conversation was headed, but I kept myself quiet. 'How do you manage keeping yourself satisfied? What about your needs? You jolly well need someone for that job. I'm forty-two and it becomes harder, you want it more.'

I just looked at her and said with a smile, 'Yes, for sure.' The one burning desire on everyone's mind, the ultimate goal of satisfaction: sex! Yes! Why not? That is the totality that drives every creature. Not love, not feelings, just unadulterated sex.

'Hey! My college friend from Sydney is coming to Delhi, we'll be throwing a small party. Why don't you come? I'll let you know soon.' I was hesitant to say yes, but the only way to escape any kind of persuasion was simply by saying, 'Yes!'. Somewhat similar to me, she was astonishingly outspoken and embarrassingly personal.

***

The next morning after class, everything looked a bit mundane. Baba was pre-occupied with his business and Maa was quietly cleaning her bedroom cupboard. There was no balcony for me to stand in and take in the outside world. I was too frustrated to even kill time. How did Maa manage, day after day? Was it her patience or was it by choice? I was getting angry and perhaps I should've tried to make more friends at the centre.

By now I was getting agitated and sat on the sofa like a teenager, waiting to explode in tears. What did I want to do? I didn't know. I now stood between contemplation and regret, or would it be right to say condemnation of my own judgment in making decisions? I was thinking aloud, regretting being here.

'Why don't you watch TV?' Maa said to me politely and I just sneered at her. I was rude and sat there quietly. She made some tea and asked me to join her. I just took the cup of tea and went back to my sofa. 'What is wrong with you? Why are you so quiet?' Maa asked; Baba asked the same question.

'No, Nothing!' was my response. I didn't want to get into an argument by expressing what I felt, otherwise they'd feel I was blaming them for feeling this way. They wouldn't understand and would jump to conclusions without reasoning (from my point of view). It was better to keep my mouth shut.

I just needed to be alone with my thoughts. But they were my parents and I knew them well; they wouldn't stop niggling until they got the answer they were looking for. I'm not a parent but I do understand that Indian parents care about their children a bit too much – sometimes it's overbearing.

I may have been overreacting because I'd been on my own much too long, and I'd been criticised by Baba before for that, when I drowned in my sorrows, alone in a room. He had mentioned to Maa once, 'She is so used to living alone that she loves to be alone, even here with her own people, so she locks herself all day in that room.' He made the point loud and clear so I could hear it.

I wanted to avoid condemnation today, so I quietly slipped into my room and started writing in my notebook.

Lunch was quiet and sombre too. Maa insisted I have a bit more of the fish and I was quiet. She started saying, 'So you are not happy to be with us here?'

'Maa, why are you starting something that has no meaning at all? Will it make you happy if I say I'm happy?'

Baba signalled to Maa to say no more.

I hurriedly finished my lunch and went into my room. I wanted to cry but I was too angry. I just needed space and I guess that was too much to ask. They wouldn't rest until it was resolved. I wanted to avoid the drama, the speculation and the justifications, but it stretched like chewing gum. Maybe, part of it was my fault – I was stretching the situation. Maa wasn't far behind; she could've just left me to cool myself down.

That afternoon, I finally cried. No one forced me to come here; I was here on my own terms, but I wasn't living my life. I felt this way because I wanted to feel sorry for myself and blame everyone. I didn't go out because I didn't have friends, stipulating that if I made new friends, they would feel sad or hurt that I didn't find their company too appealing, and I was scared to be judged again by my own parents.

I slept until it was time for afternoon tea. I got up worse than before and ready to attack any sarcasm without any second thought.

I sat with a grumpy face, slowly sipping my tea; Maa came close and sat next to me with her tea. From the corner of my eye, I could see that she was looking at me. I was waiting for her to say something – I knew she would, but the question was when.

I was about to go for a biscuit when she finally spoke. 'I am your Maa, so don't try to hide from me. What exactly is the matter with you? Has anyone said anything to you, or have we said something without knowing?'

By this time, I was feeling guilty, but I was too stubborn to admit it or to apologise for my behaviour. I was quiet.

During dinner, Maa started another conversation. 'Why don't you go out for a walk in the evening? I could join you.'

I couldn't stop myself from saying something; in fact, I tried to be polite, but I guess I wasn't, otherwise I wouldn't have infuriated Baba. 'Where will I go? If I go out, there are thousands of questions. Don't wear this, don't do that, don't wear that. You're busy with your temple. Where will you go out with me? I don't make friends here because of you.' Finally, I said it aloud. I didn't think about the consequences but just said it. It did sound as if I was blaming them. Anger is a very bad thing – it makes us different people.

'You're old enough to understand you shouldn't be speaking to your Maa like that. We never stop you from going anywhere or tell you what to do.' Baba was raising his voice by now. 'We never asked you to come here in the first place. You do something terrible in life and you blame other people.'

Still angry, I managed to say to Baba, 'I'm not blaming anyone, but it seems no one tries to understand what I'm trying to say here.' This was now leading to a massive argument; I could feel it in his voice.

'If you're not blaming anyone, what was that? You just said it. Since this morning you're sulking. You're not talking, just quiet as if it's our fault.'

'Baba, all I need is space; I go through this spasm of momentary aloofness. You leave me for a while and I'll be okay. Sadly, it seems no one understands what I want. I'm your daughter – at least you should have understood?'

'You make mistakes and then you cry over it when you regret. You expect us to understand you? Have you ever tried to understand us or help us understand your problems? You just look at yourself, selfishly trying to make your life sad – and when regrets sets in, you try to repent.'

I felt myself burning with anger and tears were welling up. I left my food and looked away from my plate, to hide my tears. Maa was asking Baba to be quiet. He was speaking the truth and making me realise my mistakes. Sometimes truth is sharper than any weapon in the world; it bites you so hard that the wounds remain open forever. I softly said to him, now with tears slowly dropping from my eyes, 'So, you think it's my fault. I'm to be blamed for everything?'

He was very angry with me. 'Yes! I'm very ashamed to have a daughter like you. You are responsible for your own actions and it would have been better if I did not have a daughter like you at all.'

I pushed the plate away, ran to my room and closed it. I went to the bathroom and slapped myself with cold water, as if I was in a bad dream and the cold water would wake me up. All it was doing was washing away the tears. I couldn't differentiate between water and tears anymore.

My past, my life, was now catching up with me. I must have really hurt Babạ. He seldom spoke but when he did, he was always blunt. I had made a few wrong decisions in life, but had he ever tried to understand me?

Me! That's what was eating me up inside. Perhaps I always thought about myself and never tried to understand how I would affect others. But aren't experiences supposed to make people strong? People have to go through these experiences to become a better person. Maybe I've always seen my sorrows more openly and have forgotten to see theirs.

Maybe Baba was right: I was not a good daughter. But I was also just an ordinary human being; perhaps Baba failed to see that before branding me as a bad daughter. He had his share of experiences, some bad and some good. I always thought of him as an extraordinary person. He was a good human being, a good father. I would complain about life sometimes but never directly to him.

I always thought if I hadn't done this or done that, what would my life have been like? I was getting tired, analysing life too much, so I prayed. 'Show me a way. I want relief from this punishment.'

I must have dozed off as when I opened my eyes, I could hear Jethu filling the water, so it was five in the morning. Light was seeping through the curtains.

I got up to dress to go to Poonam's, still overwhelmed by yesterday's argument with Baba. I quietly snuck outside. Once I was there, Poonam was talking to her mother on the mobile and she waved at me. I was there early, quarter to seven in the morning. Yoga would start every day around seven in the morning.

She looked at my long face and asked me, 'Why is my clown not smiling today?'

I just smiled dryly. 'Had an argument. Father and I had a bit of a conflict of interest. He thinks differently than me.' I didn't want to indulge her more, so I was hesitant and chose my words carefully. I just managed to say, 'Maybe I didn't let them get close to me, or they didn't try to close the gap. Perhaps the bridge was burned from both sides and none of us felt the need to ask why?' I was looking at the floor, trying not to break into tears.

Poonam was intelligent enough not to ask more. 'Parents are the foundation on which we children stand, dance, cry and hug. I want the smile, my clown! Go and give your dad a big hug, you will see, everything will be alright.'

I nodded and for a brief moment I wanted to hold back my tears, but I let it loose.

Poonam hugged me. 'Keep smiling, no matter how dark! You think it's bad today but there's always light tomorrow! I started this place ten years ago, not realising that there are a lot of women like me who want some kind of happiness. I had a fantastic childhood, I was always a tomboy. My parents always gave me the freedom to do whatever I wanted to do but they were strict too; my dad was in the army. So, we had to move from one place to the other when he was reposted. It was hard to get into the life of one town and leave it to embrace the other. But I adjusted with time. I was stubborn and had my way. I played the role of a good daughter – and when I got married, a good wife, and then a good mother.

'Then one day I thought, everyone is busy with their lives – my husband with his business and my children with their studies, what about me? I didn't have any escape, so I built this as my peace, and I tried to relate to the women here – or, you can say, vice versa.

'I wanted middle-class women to come here; they can forget their world and just lose themselves here for a few hours. We wanted to be each other's strength and depend on each other's sorrows and happiness. This is the way we women are. We see strength in connection, no matter how independent we are and how strong.'

Poonam continued, 'Money is not everything; I didn't start this place for money. Well, initially I did, but then slowly I understood money is important, but it cannot be the main purpose. I don't keep a record of who pays and who doesn't. It's not a business, it's more than a business. I wanted to attain life without profit or loss. People can say it's a business, but through these women I've learned so much. Am I happy? Maybe, or I don't know. I write articles in the newspapers and I go to schools to give lectures on life and women. Why? Because I value it and this is my passion. I started The Missing Peace.'

I interrupted Poonam. 'The Missing Peace? What's that?'

Poonam looked at me, surprised. 'You don't know?' She smiled and took out what looked to be an invoice; on the top was written 'The Missing Peace'. Then she said, 'This place is called The Missing Peace. Oh, how would you know? I don't advertise! I don't need to anymore, and as it's in a residential place, no one is allowed to advertise. I was missing something in life. I witnessed love, marriage and children. When I became a mother, I wasn't happy. Don't get me wrong, I love my children more than anything in this world. I just didn't know how to react then, what to do and then I involved myself in them and found happiness, the joy to be a mother. The same way I found my happiness again, involving myself in the life of others. I involved myself in these women, as if there sorrows and happiness are mine. They identified themselves with me, and me with them; this is how I get my daily rush of peace.'

I smiled at her. She was amazing indeed.

'I get calls from parents, "please guide my daughter", or, "Aunty, guide me on what profession to choose". There was this girl who came here, her husband used to beat her. One day she did the inevitable – she ran away. She had no place to go, being new in town, and she was petrified. She came to me and I gave her a place to stay in my house. I fought with my husband and everyone just to keep her, because I believed in her and I cannot see suffering. She is fine now, with a good job, and she writes a letter every now and then. She has a life now.' Poonam smiled. 'So, my dear, smile. Life is made up of these small bumps. You just had an argument with your dad; every daughter has it with their father. You are no different.'

I realised what she was trying to tell me, and I felt a sense of calm – or perhaps her peace was slowly engulfing me with charm. We hugged each other and soon the girls of 'The Missing Peace' came one by one.

She was starting her class and it was 7.10 already – no sign of the yoga teacher. she was late. I quietly sat behind Poonam's class to watch the girls of The Missing Peace with a pair of fresh eyes.

Poonam said to all the girls, 'Before we start the class, could we pray in silence for two minutes for Shweta's mother, who just had an operation.' I later learned that Shweta's mother's leg had to be amputated. I didn't ask why; it was something private. Poonam prayed, 'Please give strength and perseverance to Shweta and her mother at this time of crisis. May peace and happiness be with you both.' Shortly after this, everyone was hugging her. I didn't know her but when I saw her, I felt her strength. She wasn't crying or complaining; she was here with the girls, getting on with her life – and me, I was crying for a little tussle with Baba.

Are relationships so fragile? Why there is so much of blaming? Children and parents should understand each other, not fight among themselves to prove a point. Maybe I was the weakest link; maybe I didn't make the effort for them to come close to me. They were always there. Maybe I didn't extend my hand, when they always extended theirs. I was engulfed with myself and didn't feel the urge to involve them in my loneliness; perhaps they got tired and stopped trying.

I didn't do yoga or the sessions with Poonam; instead I watched them and just sat there. Jerry made a joke or two as well. Finally, I was with Astha and Poonam in Astha's car.

At home, I was welcomed by my friends, the dog family. I stood there for a brief moment, thinking of how to go inside and apologise for my behaviour to Baba. I was stubborn – but Poonam's words were making it impossible for me to neglect Baba, and it was all true. Love doesn't make a person small or big by apologising. It's all about understanding. I failed to understand Baba's sorrow, his point of view as a father.

I went straight into my room. I felt guilty for being the person who stood there just feeling sorry for herself.

Khokhon bought in my tea. 'Here, Didi, have some tea, you barely had dinner last night. Do you want biscuits?'

'No thanks, I'll be fine.' Maybe the tea would refresh my mind before I spoke to Baba.

I was just about to take my first sip when Baba entered the room. 'You did not wake me up? Now that's not good. You should have.' He was rubbing his hand on my head. 'Dearest, life is made of happiness and tears. Both walk hand in hand. Sometimes you will get the shadows of the sun and sometimes there will be burning heat. I'm sorry, dear. I love you and sometimes I feel you have taken yourself so far from us that we cannot reach you. Why? We are all with you.'

I was numb, speechless and perhaps embarrassed. I was now in tears.

'Don't break down, if you cry, I will cry too. Because of you children, we try to find ourselves and happiness. Don't give up now. I'm always with you. If you hurt or get hurt, I will be feeling the same pain – you are my child, after all.' He sat beside me, and we wiped each others' tears.

'Sorry Baba, I know I must have hurt you and Maa, but I just couldn't help it.'

'I understand your sorrows, your loneliness … but give us a chance to come close to you. Now come on, come in the lounge, and sit with us.'

I sent a text to Poonam: 'We children are our parents' dreams and through our eyes they search their dreams. Dreams of happiness that they once saw when they were young. Through them we start to believe in all that is in life to believe. From the moment we take our first walk to the day we start our lives. We made up!'

The next morning, I flashed a big smile at Poonam. 'That's my girl,' she said.

'Poonam, what is happiness? I don't know. I thought I would be happy here with my parents. I even resigned from my job. Why am I here? I feel more lost than ever.'

'Hmm ... you've made up with your dad but not with yourself. Never mind! My dear, you cannot get happiness just by changing places. You first have to know what you want. We search for dependency and we mistake that for happiness. Where do you belong? You first have to answer that. You have to rest yourself, love yourself and then you will find your own way.'

I was more confused than before. I didn't tell Poonam the entire story of my life – but she could be right. My own loneliness led me into the hands of men who also were in search of themselves; ultimately, it led to my own destruction at the hands of a blackmailer.

I told Poonam bits and pieces and she looked at me, saying, 'You were lonely and for you to be with men was your escapism ... in that ordeal, you forgot to take a good look at yourself and the men you were involved with. I wouldn't say you were naïve but sometimes these things happen for a reason.'

I would agree with Poonam to some extent, but I was in search for love. Sometimes familial love is not enough – or perhaps they were so caught up chasing their dreams, they just saw me as an active participant and forgot to see me as an individual. In some way, it was my fault too. I was over-thinking again. I was waiting for the yoga class to start and I promised myself I would be more present today.

It was the usual Surya Namaskar and all of us were huffing and puffing when one of the women said, 'We Indian women are obsessed with losing weight. So, what do we do? Yoga with you here in the morning for ourselves, yoga at bed with our husband at night and yoga in the kitchen for the family! I have dancing rotis now.' We all started laughing. Friend looked at me and said, 'Come over tonight, my friend from Sydney is cooking Mexican. It will be a small get-together. Here is my number.'

I quickly added it to my contact list on my phone. 'What do you like to drink? If it's Mexican, then maybe chardonnay?'

Friend said, 'Just come, there'll be plenty to drink and eat. We're going shopping at INA Market.'

***

'Maa, I have to go to this party, with this girl I befriended at the yoga place.' I felt the urge to ask for permission.

Maa looked at me, keeping her teacup down, and said, 'Is it important for you to go?'

'Manju, don't. Of course you should go. I will drop you off, just tell me when,' Baba addressed both me and Maa.

I wasn't sure if I wanted to go out or not, but the other half of me was looking forward to the evening. I got my jumpsuit and my jewellery out to wear. After a very long time, I was making an effort to get dressed.

Maa came to my room and explained that she was happy I was going out. I think she had more to say, but I understood her without her saying anything at all.

She is my mother and I'm her daughter. Perhaps she wanted me not to go, as in Melbourne I had so many friends and I was always with them, around them, in their lives (and they in mine). Now that I was here, she wanted me to be with her – a bit possessive, a bit lonely and scared to lose me again.

I went to Friend's place with a box of pastries. I was greeted by her twenty-year-old daughter and twelve-year-old son. I was surprised to see this; Friend looked incredibly young to have a grown-up daughter. They looked like identical twins. After nonstop compliments – which I had forgotten how to handle lately – I finally sat on her couch.

I was introduced to her friend, whom I learned was a painter from Sydney – I just thought of her as 'Friend'. She had returned to India to start her life from scratch. Jerry was there too with her husband and her two sons – it was quite a pleasant evening.

With a riesling in my hand, I was enjoying the first sip of alcohol after several months.

'So, you like it here?' I asked 'Painter from Sydney'. I just wanted to start a conversation.

She smiled and said, 'Yes! Love it. Just love it. I'm planning to stay here by the end of this year for good. What about you? Do you like it here?'

I didn't know what to say at first. 'Melbourne is a good place …'

Then Jerry asked Painter from Sydney to join her in the balcony for a smoke. She asked me and I politely declined; I was very tempted to, but I lied that I don't smoke. I don't know why; was I trying to be someone else? Soon, after a few other conversations with people around the room, I joined Jerry as Painter from Sydney ran to the kitchen to check on her tacos.

'It's great you could make it tonight. You need a break sometimes. Everyone needs a break now and then. Don't you get bored sometimes of doing nothing? I do and I can't see myself sitting still for one minute.'

I smiled at Friend and asked her about her mother-in-law, whom I saw from the balcony coming out of her room to give her regards to the people in the room.

'After my husband passed away, I didn't know what to do and wanted to take my designing career to the next level. So I started this business and now I'm exporting to five countries in Europe. I live for myself and my children. You can call it my escapism.' She smiled and lit another cigarette. 'I've organised everything for my mother-in-law: a TV in the room, a maid. I don't want her to cross my path, or me her path. We are distant but to the world we are so close. She used to hurt me with words, but each and every word of hers made me strong – so strong that sometimes I say thank you to her … only in my prayers.' We both smiled, she took another puff and continued, 'My husband left me with this flat and a lot of grievances. I'm happy.'

'I'm sorry, I didn't know about your husband.'

'It's okay, I never told you.'

'And I never asked.'

Friend smiled. 'Look at him.' She pointed out a guy who was also a designer, working for a multinational brand. 'He's gay! He can't tell the world how he feels and what he wants; he can't even share this with his parents. He lives a secret life – daily he dies in silence. Most importantly, the world knows he has a girlfriend. Our society is so ugly that it cannot accept anything beautiful. Jealous! Perhaps the person in this society does not have love. Isn't it funny the way we accept the world, no matter how ugly and beautiful it is? Yet, we humans cannot have any ugliness in the people we love around us. We condemn their ugliness, torturing them into being plastic.'

Once inside I looked at the array of food in front of me. I had a large bite of my taco. It was okay. Jerry was a strict vegetarian, so Friend had to let go of any kind of meat produce. The guacamole was okay, not that good and not that bad. The people in the room silently looked at each other and chuckled. Friend and Painter from Sydney were juggling between balcony, living room and the kitchen entertaining guests.

Jerry said quietly to all of us, 'Say it's delicious, otherwise we would hurt her feelings. She's too proud of her cooking.'

At this, everyone burst into little giggles and Painter from Sydney rushed in from the kitchen with a serious face, asking how the food was. Everyone in unison said, 'Very good!' Jerry, who was running after her two-year-old, was laughing away. 'Friend' still didn't get it and she was now showing an imperfect way of eating tacos. I was struck with awe by her principles of physics, applied to these poor tacos. I tried to eat them slowly, mindful of not breaking the tacos before they reached my mouth, just to save myself from Friend's lecture.

I slowly made my way to the couch with my tacos and between the hustle and bustle of the taco disaster, I was looking at all the amazing people in the room. Everyone was somewhere and they were a little lonely, but somehow still content. They were somewhat unhappy but they still didn't forget to live.

***

I was once again in my room, writing in my journal. Ranju, our maid, came in for sweeping. She always addressed me as Didi and my mother as Maa – after all, she *is* 'Maa'. Ranju was twenty-five years old, tall, slim and very attractive. Her face had seen the many struggles of life – the lines in her face were testament to this. She was polite yet outspoken, but always with a smile. She had four daughters aged thirteen, twelve, nine and six years old.

Her husband worked interstate in Punjab as the head of a machinery unit. He came to visit them during Holi but due to some arguments with Ranju over his drinking problems, he fought with her and left. It had been one and half months since that incident. Sometimes he would send money but sometimes he didn't. Ranju was today's strong Indian woman; she didn't just wait in anxiety to hear from him or for his money. She worked in four houses, one of them ours and another one belonging to a teacher who promised Ranju that she would help with the admission process for her youngest child in the nearby government school.

She was busy during the day and she couldn't afford education for her elder daughter. In government schools, education is free up to high school. Ranju mentioned that after the school holidays she would like her to continue with her studies. So she was working hard.

Ranju wanted her daughter to do some household work, like cleaning and dusting. She asked Maa to keep her at our place for a few hours. I fought with Maa not to give in to her request. She was only thirteen! Maa looked at the situation differently; she thought that by giving her the job, she would be helping Ranju financially. I was not convinced with this philosophy, so I tried telling her to visualise me when I was thirteen and if I was doing this work.

Her reply was, 'If it's not us, it will be someone else, and then you would never know their plight.'

I was adamant and somehow Baba agreed with me – and that was the end of the subject. Maa took a back step; two against one was very hard for her to win.

I learned later that Ranju kept her daughter nearby, next to the teacher's flat. She was looking after a two year old baby and helping the baby's mother around the house for three hours every day. I was devastated. I said to Ranju, 'What was the need?'

Ranju quietly set the broom on the floor and sat beside me, folding her legs next to the bed. 'Didi, I have four daughters; I cannot afford all their education, no matter how much I want them to study. In a few years I have to think about their marriage too. I cannot depend on their father, can I? If I had a son, things would have been quite different. I married early so every two years I was made pregnant, just in the hope for a son.

'After my youngest was born, I decided not to have any more children and my mother-in-law was somewhat supportive, but the hope of a grandson always made her sad. Sometimes she would pester me to get pregnant and show her annoyance towards me. There was a doctor in our village hospital camp, and she advised me to take contraceptive pills. She told me if I didn't stop making babies, my life would be at risk.'

I asked Ranju her opinion. She looked at me as if no one had asked her that question before. 'Didi, to me – girl or boy, it doesn't matter. They're all equal and it's not in my hand.'

I smiled and asked, 'Did you ever want a son?'

She looked at me sadly and now her voice was soft. 'A couple of years ago, I was still in the village. One day I had a severe stomach ache and went to the hospital camp. It was over crowded and the doctor was very busy but still saw me. She examined and told me I was twelve weeks pregnant, and I was putting my life at risk. She asked me to get my husband next day. So we were advised to abort the child and to that, we both agreed. I was given a medicine. I had the pill and Didi, you won't believe what happened. I was in so much pain.'

I interrupted Ranju, 'Why didn't she operate?'

'She advised me that it wasn't needed and in a village like ours, maybe we didn't have the facility or … I don't know, I did what I was told to do. My body felt as if it was not mine and something was trying to come out. My oldest daughter was so scared. I asked her to fetch her father from the fields. I remember seeing drops of blood coming from my vagina and something fell. I don't remember what happened after that, as I was unconscious. When I woke up I was in a pool of blood and my husband was crying … he had a small foetus which looked like that of a boy.'

I could see her tears by now and I too felt goose bumps. I felt tears slowly dripping from my eyes. I hugged her so tightly and in that moment I felt her sorrows, so exasperating against the miracles of God.

'I saw his little hands and feet, not fully developed but I saw them. Next day I had to clean the blood and couldn't forgive myself.'

I looked at Ranju and said to her strongly, 'It was not your fault; you had to do this because you had to live for yourself and your daughters. You're sad because you had a son and I don't think you would have been that sad if it was a girl.'

'Maybe you're right Didi, but I was sad to see a life that I had produced in that state. That time, maybe I was angry because I got what I wanted after so many years and then it was taken away from me this way, for my safety. For a very long time I felt I killed it for my selfishness, but then I realised it was not my fault and it happened for a reason. I now live for my daughters and in them I see that little foetus. It makes me strong.'

I nodded and was rubbing away my tears when Maa walked into the room. 'Will there be any work done today or not?'

Ranju started laughing and said, 'It's all Didi's fault, she got me in a trance and we started talking.' She started sweeping the room and when she went to sweep Maa's room, I told Maa her story.

When Maa heard this, she was also very sad but then she said, 'The poor have no choice, and they cannot make any choices – they don't have a right, just a right to live. So don't pity her, she is a strong woman. If you pity her, she will embrace her poverty and will do nothing about it.'

The purpose of me writing this is we are in 2011 and we are still talking how important it is to have a son in the family. Why girls are not looked as the future. The future belongs to us females. We give birth, nurture and educate.

I used to look at Ranju as a weak woman who had succumbed to the economics of the world. But she wasn't different to any woman in the world. She cried when she wanted to and laughed when she wanted to. Poverty had nothing to do with it. She was working hard to make ends meet. In front of me stood a strong woman of modern India. Though she might have studied until grade five, her knowledge about life was superior to any textbooks or classroom lectures.

To save herself from people's pity, she didn't act as a victim. She was not only fulfilling her duties as a mother to her daughters, but also secretly fulfilling her dream. Her original dream was to have a son but within her daughters, she found her new dream. It was a simple dream, a dream of having a simple life. The simple life came in food, water, shelter, clothing – and a little bit of money to buy these things – and within that happiness, a bit of basic education.

 # DIARIES OF ME

Marriage to me was unknown territory; how could I pass on my judgment of Ranju to someone who was as callous as me? I wanted to escape this torture, but I couldn't, as I was already into this without my consent.

I was beginning to think about Thomas and Amit. So many failed relationships, but was it my fault entirely? How could I grasp the whole idea of marriage and advise someone like Ranju? I wasn't ready for anything and this situation was sounding to me as fictitious as marriage. It was not my marriage!

Before I met Amit and after my divorce, I was consumed by the whole idea of losing weight. I thought this would be a stepping-stone to falling in love with myself. Sadly, that became an obsessive idea, nothing to do with falling in love with myself. I was so obsessed with it that I started to believe losing weight would make me so beautiful that I would attract men. I forgot that bones only attracted dogs. In fact, Amit took advantage of my obsession and it soon became his dream that I was living in.

I was so engulfed by it that I forgot I was living someone else's life again. If someone asked me what was so common between the two of us – why I loved him so much – I wouldn't know what to say. He would sneer at me for eating too much and lecture me on how chocolates could be bad for me. Compliments were alien to me; it all depended on his mood. He would scold me as if I was two years old if I spoke too much or in a loud voice, or if the food I cooked turned out to be very plain. Sometimes he would reward me with an ice-cream if I behaved properly. Often, I tried to compare him with Thomas, but they were two different people.

He came to find peace with me with his broken heart. During the course of the relationship, I became dependent on him. The more he ignored me, the more I wanted him. Was it love? I don't know – at that time, maybe it was. He would often make me brush my teeth twice, otherwise he wouldn't kiss me. For him, making love with me was only for his pure satisfaction; either he didn't know how to do it, or he didn't want to. On earlier occasions, it was like a five-minute thrust of bodies. He never knew what I wanted, and he never asked. He would force me to go down on him and not once would he ask if that's what I wanted.

To overcome this shallow, foul play of lovemaking, I would fake every orgasm so I could be done with this obscene, vulgar torture of impropriety. One day I tried reverse psychology on him and asked him to go down on me, but he responded with, 'Yuck!' I tried to convince him with the same understanding. He would then behave like a little boy deprived of his favourite toy. He would pinch me, pull my hair and slap me so hard that I had to give in to his odd persuasive ways.

Once, I forgot to take the pill. We were at the movies when he asked again and I was familiar with his anger, so I said a little white lie. But when he decided to have sex, I couldn't lie anymore: I told him the truth. He grabbed me by my hair and slammed me into the car window. He drove so fast that he skipped the lights and when he reached my apartment, the car was still on and he screamed at me to get out!

I still gave in to him when he apologised, but he made it a point that I apologise too. To him, it was my fault.

I never stopped him going out with his friends; he had all the freedom he wanted. I, on the other hand, never had that; if I wanted to go out, he would then make his plans suddenly clash with me and I had to cancel. Sometimes to hide his guilt he would say to me that I should go out more often.

He would often ask me not to call him during these times or send any text messages. I was getting tired of his insinuations and insults. One day, when he seemed to be in a rather good mood, I asked him where we stood. He couldn't answer; he just left. We later had a massive fight on the phone. I felt cheated when he couldn't answer a simple question.

I wanted to stop what I was feeling; I was suffocating with his hate for me. My mind was racing like a car without any brakes, until I took refuge in sleeping pills and vertigo medication. I wasn't answering phones; knowing something was wrong, my sister rushed to my aid. I was taken to the hospital.

The next day, Amit visited me; he had no sympathy for me. He was cold and calculated in choosing his words. I just tried to hold his hands to apologise but he pushed me away, saying, 'That's the way you grab attention. Why did you do this to torture me? What will you get from all of this? I tried to tell you, we cannot be anything, but you had to force your love on me.'

He didn't give me the chance to apologise, but after being accused of forcing myself upon him, I became quiet. I didn't argue, nor did I try to stop him. I let him go as quickly as I welcomed him in my life.

Once, I was at lunch with a colleague, Siddhant. I was happy to go out for a change, to meet people again – but boys will be boys, men will be men. A slight hint of weakness and they will take advantage of the situation. Not all men are like this. It's not right to blame anyone; I was equally responsible. I didn't ask for pity, nor did I stop him from kissing me. It was soothing to feel someone's affection and feel wanted again. I was as human as Siddhant was and I was only responding to an act of infatuation or affection. I don't know. I quickly withdrew myself from him, thinking how wrong it was. I felt guilty about betraying Amit.

I didn't know at that time that the universe was conspiring against me. Amit called me after a few days and without thinking, I welcomed him back. I thought he'd changed. He took care of me and was slowly participating in every little thing in my life, but I never thought that it was the beginning of an end. I felt guilty for kissing Siddhant and sometimes truth can be harder to accept; knowing how Amit was, I hid it. I just couldn't afford to lose Amit again. I covered my guilt with his love.

I moved to South Yarra to be close to him and for the first time in three years, he took me to his house, showering me with gifts on my birthday. Then he left for India to visit his parents.

The day he left for India, there was a huge terrorist attack in Mumbai; the news made headlines around the world, with terrorists opening fire on the streets of Mumbai. Loved ones were instantly lost in just a span of hours from the bullets of evil. I felt sad and uncomfortable with this news; I tried to reflect on life and called my parents to hear their voices. I even tried contacting Amit's mobile to hear his voice – for him to tell me he was okay.

Amit wanted some money and I gave it to him, not thinking for once that he would be lost forever.

I forced him to meet my parents – maybe it was not required, but at that point it felt right. He wasn't happy for me to contact him in India and would often scream at me on the phone. He returned to Melbourne as a different man. I still didn't get the hint. He was talking of going to Singapore to meet his friends in the next month; he'd just come back from India, why did he have to go and visit his friends again? But he did.

It was Sudha, my Indian friend, who told me to look at Orkut (almost like the Indian counterpart of Facebook). I quickly logged in and searched his name. There it was in black and white. He was arm in arm with her. I checked her relationship status and she was in a relationship with him.

I was numb and angry. I wanted to confront him and then wondered if there was any point in me arguing with him. I did; I screamed at him and then begged him to answer me – where was my fault in all of this? I begged him to love me. I just asked him one thing: why couldn't he be honest with me, why all the lies and deception? He had all the excuses in the world, as if I was blowing things out of proportion. It was the end. He was so weak that he couldn't tell me once.

Over the years, he borrowed my laptop and he returned it to me when it was broken. He used and discarded me just like the laptop. I tried to fix the laptop; it took three hundred dollars. But what about my heart? How many dollars would it require to mend it?

The laptop found not only his mysterious life, but also secret love letters to her and a lot of photos of his other girlfriends. I was a nobody. He should've had the decency to delete them – but he did not. I was so angry I called Amit, warning him if he did anything more to hurt me, then I would contact his new friend in India to tell her what kind of man he was. I didn't feel any regret sending a friend request to her.

The phone call I received that night was an open field of abusive language from Amit. I didn't stop; I was fearless and told him if he ever contacted me again, then it would result badly. He got shaken up with just one tap on his shoulder. What about those millions of abuses that I took from him day and night? They didn't mean anything to him.

We parted ways and a big part of me departed with him. Since then, I'd been walking in and out of relationships with uncertainty. I wasn't thinking, not giving a moment to myself to analyse my situation. I stopped breathing. I embraced any kind of affection that was bestowed upon me, forgetting that it was doing me more harm than good. I was begging to be loved, and in return all I got was men taking advantage of the situation, using me like an object. Every seduction had betrayal written on it.

Siddhant and I crossed paths again and this time he had an open invitation to sleep with me. No love involved, just pure sex! Somehow, I rose above that temptation, only to succumb to another. I was turning into another person. Was I searching for Amit or myself?

I don't blame them, as there's nothing to blame. I could've blamed Amit, but what difference was there between him and me? It was my grieving period and I handled it my way. Every seduction and every moment felt like I was punishing myself for everything that happened. I thought it would be easy for me to forget Amit. I was oblivious to my own circumstances.

Over time, Amit would call and I would hang up. One day we talked, but I was being very arrogant and everything I said was filled with sarcasm. He hung up!

It was after eight months, in November when I was travelling to India to visit my parents, when he called. A part of me still loved him so I spoke to him. He came to visit me because I allowed him to. He was giving his explanation about him and the 'other' woman, that there was nothing between them, and I just blew things out of proportion. He did try to cross the line, but I had things under control this time. I pushed him away and told him it's not happening again. He went home and called me; it was somewhat like the old days but different. I wondered whether it would be wise to welcome him as a friend, or whether it would be a mistake. The following months revealed the mysteries.

After his visit and phone call, I texted him and soon he was replying to those messages. Once in India I texted him back in Melbourne – he didn't reply. Later he called me only to abuse me. I was lost but the more he abused me, the more I wanted him because I still loved him.

Once back in Melbourne, entering the flat was like a slow process of being killed by loneliness. I called Amit. He came to visit me and we both had dinner. It didn't take much time for him to persuade me to be intimate.

I felt terrible and with trepidation I asked him where all this was leading to, when he called me that night. His cold voice filled the phone. I was shaking, as this was beginning to feel like history repeating its torture. He said the same thing over and over again: that he was a bit lonely so he couldn't control himself. That was his excuse – what was mine? Was I as guilty as him? Was I guilty of falling in love with him again or did I just want to pacify my loneliness? I begged him – but for what? To love me? Or to continue to abuse me? Was I abusing myself? I had only questions and no answers.

Weeks and then months went – and then on Valentine's Day, I was with the girls at Anthea's farmhouse when Amit called. I was surprised and thought that perhaps I shouldn't have come with the girls – maybe he was coming back. I was guilty of such thoughts.

Two weeks later, I got a call from Amit again; this time he wanted to see me. I tried to stop but I welcomed him back again.

I remember that day very well; it will go down in history with me. Who knew that day was the start of an end, and the beginning of my destruction?

I thought he'd changed. He was apologetic enough to make me decide that it was okay to welcome him back again. I got the call on my mobile when I was walking home from work and was contemplating if it was the right thing to do – but it was too late and under the shadows of love, I started to believe in him again.

I'd just finished cooking dinner when he came, engulfing me in a massive hug. His hands were all over my face, and while kissing me he slowly moved his hands to my breasts. He wanted me to respond but I couldn't move. I became numb. He looked at me and said, 'I am here.' That had a hypnotic effect on my senses and rest was history.

I didn't know if we were making love or having sex but it was like the old times – and suddenly he pushed me away after his climax. Amit got up and dressed, ordering me to get his dinner as he was getting late. He was again that arrogant man I fell in love with. I feared today would be a repeat of history.

He ate and left without a word, just a quick peck on the cheek. He left me with the dishes around the sink and a bittersweet taste of the past. I was nervous to ask him anything, even though I had to – but when? Amit called that night to say goodnight and like old times, I was asked not to call him back again. He was back to his controlling and twisted ways.

The next day at work, I felt lost and couldn't quite fathom what was happening again. I was floating in my body but with a dead soul. I looked at the mobile: no text messages. I waited to go home and speak to him.

I couldn't tell anyone what happened; everyone in my family despised him, and my friends would be hurt if I told them, because they had always warned me. Issy would've been the most hurt, but I told her bits and pieces. I told her only what I wanted to tell, forgetting that good friends never judge, they help. But help is only given to those who help themselves. I was destroying myself with Amit again.

When I had the courage, I called Amit. After the normal 'how was your day' and greeting, I buckled up some courage to talk to him. 'Amit, where are we heading to again?'

Amit was silent and then he laughed. 'Heading to where? Oh! About last night, that was nothing. I came to see you but when I see you, I get carried away. You were a bit lonely and so was I. We are nothing.' Amit was blunt and cold.

My body trembled with anger and I felt a teardrop or two. I felt dirty, sweet-talked into an act of rape. I screamed at him, 'Amit, you have no right to play with my emotions like this. What am I to you? Did you ever respect me? Why do you always do this to me, why? I'm a human and I have feelings. What fun do you get from torturing me?' He was quiet. 'Why do you hate me so much? Why can't you love me, is sex all you need? You could've gone to a brothel!'

Finally, he spoke to cover his guilt. 'You consented to it last night; I didn't force you, did I? I have other commitments, this is nothing.'

There, he said it. I felt like a fool; I hated his guts and despised my own instincts. I couldn't hear anything he was saying, I was so absorbed in myself. I hung up to cry the tears of betrayal.

Today, I was not only a victim of his physical rape, but I was raped of my trust. It was a rape of my love. I rubbed my tears and called my sister, not to get her pity or sympathy but because I had to let go of the guilt that Amit placed on me. Surprisingly, she wasn't angry with me; she gave me courage and told me to be reasonable with myself.

I was so tired with all the tears that I drifted into sleep. Later, the phone rang. It was Amit. He was screaming on the phone about abusing him through my sister. I had no idea what he was saying – then I remembered she took Amit's phone number from me. I was defenseless. I didn't know what to say but I told him I'd speak to her and get back to him.

I called Sumi and she was angry that he was bothering me. She told me that she did it to tell him that I was not alone; I had a family for support and asked him to leave me alone and not to contact me again.

I just finished the phone call from her when the phone rang again. It was Amit. He was screaming again and this time I defended my sister in and out. 'Amit, if you call me again … I don't know if it's the right moment to say or not, but there is this other woman still in your life and I know it. If you bother me again, I will send her a message, or to your sister. I will! You mark my words I will.'

'No, you are not going to do anything like that. Just think about me, you have your family here. I have no one.' He was being very manipulative and this time I wasn't buying it.

'Did you ever consider this before hurting me and cheating on her?' I said. 'Does your family know what kind of man you are? A cheap mongrel! You keep coming back into my life, turning me into someone I'm not. They'll have to know what you are. I'm fed up with your harassment, your sexual and emotional abuse.' I hung up. I was so angry I didn't know what I was saying or doing. I got out my laptop and sent a friend request to Amit's sister.

It was one in the morning when he called me again. 'I will come up and smash your face, who the hell do you think you are?' Amit was not only aggressive, but also rude and sarcastic on the phone. 'I've been with girls like you, they're not even worth a penny. You better stop sending friend requests, otherwise you will regret even knowing me.'

I was composed and calm when I finally said to him, 'This respect you have for me, Amit? I just sent a friend request; just a request, and that shook you up so much. Could you imagine how fragile you have made me? I love you too much, and I can never do anything to harm you. What I did was out of anger and foolishness. I'm sorry about that but then could you, for once, realise what you've turned me into? Every time you hurt me like this, you kill me completely. You are not only cheating on that poor girl and me but above all yourself. Just leave me.'

'Rubbish! Love? You don't know what love is, otherwise, you wouldn't do these things to humiliate me. You are a fucking liar, you bitch. You wait!'

I hung up. It was useless to speak to him and I hated every moment of myself loving him. He not only questioned my love for him, but he was a weak man, not strong enough to tell me the truth of what he wanted. He never understood my love for him.

Maybe my love wasn't strong enough to survive the heat of infidelity. He knew I always dreamt of us being together, but I never knew his philandering ways, otherwise I could've made peace with it – that was how much I loved him. If he'd only said to me that all he wanted was my body and not my soul, I would've given that to him too.

The whole night he kept calling. I didn't answer his calls; if I spoke to him, he would just threaten me again. I took the phone off the hook. But the mobile kept on ringing and finally I had to turn that off too.

When I woke up, I had ten voicemails from Amit, all disgruntled and abusive messages. When he called in the morning I didn't pick up. I detailed this incident to my sister and she gave me the courage to go to the police station and file a report. I didn't want to, but Amit wouldn't stop. I couldn't continue to live like this – I finally went to the police station. I narrated the entire truth; unfortunately, they couldn't do anything and advised me to take it to court. The constable helped me understand the intervention orders and directed me to the Melbourne Magistrates' Court. She gave me the number of the Melbourne court registrar. I took the whole day off from work and got myself involved in protecting myself from Amit.

I made time to see the registrar; she heard my entire story from the start and made an application. She guided me to legal aid and getting an interim order. I was filling out the form with Amit's details, but shaken up with what address to put. The last time we met, he was looking to move so I wasn't sure if he was still there. I always called him on his mobile and home phone numbers can be transferred. Instantly, I realised how little I knew about him, a man that I love – or loved. Things were slowly becoming past tense and I felt guilty. Was this right, what I was doing? The other voice spoke to me and said *yes, it is right*. I felt strong. I had to stop him from hurting me, but it also meant I wouldn't see him again.

I was waiting at the magistrate's court. When my name was called, my legs froze. I had to take the oath on the Bible. With courage, I answered the magistrate's questions one by one.

After my questioning I was told Amit would be asked to present his case and given a chance to speak. I was given an interim order and asked to attend the next hearing to finalise the order. Amit would be summoned and if the order wasn't served to him, then we had no chance to finalise the interim order.

There was absolute silence and then in the evening I got Amit's call, but I hung up. A couple of days later I got a call from the court and was advised that Amit couldn't be served, as no one lived there. I didn't know what to do, so I called my legal aid councillor for some advice. 'Would it be wise for me to speak to him at all?' She advised me, 'Only to the point to knowing his whereabouts.'

Then it occurred to me – his workplace. I didn't know the exact address although I knew the name of the company. But did I want to humiliate him at his work? I was hesitant but then I decided that I had to think about me for a change. This was the only way to stop Amit and make him realise that I too had the right to live and feel.

The next evening, I got a call from Amit again and this time I didn't hang up. 'Why are you doing this to me? Please don't do this, please.' How the tables had turned; all these years I begged him not to hurt me, to respect and love me, but today he was begging me. Who was I to forgive him? I couldn't take it anymore and I was exhausted. I hung up without a word.

I got a call the next night from the police station informing me that Amit had been served with a court order.

***

It was March 11, 2009. I went to the court hearing to finalise my interim intervention order. I can never forget that day. I was sitting outside the legal aid office in the court when I saw him walking out of the lift: dressed in black, unshaven and hassled. He went to the counter; the clerk said to Amit that the other party had legal aid and if he wished to take any legal help, he could. I saw him running downstairs towards the lift.

It was an hour later when I saw him upstairs in the courtroom again. Our eyes met. He looked away.

After a couple of hours, I was approached by my legal aid councillor, and advised that he could contest the order in court, so we'd see what his councillor had to say. She was telling me about the court proceedings; I was far away, thinking about Amit.

After another hour, I was told that Amit was ready to consent with admission. He would give me the intervention order but not admit to all the allegations. *What a coward*, I thought – but saying that, a thief will never say he has stolen until proven guilty. He didn't have the balls to contest me because he knew he was guilty, so this was the easy way out. My legal aid councillor asked me to agree to this, as he was ready to give his consent and finalise the intervention order. I felt that it was enough. Did he feel any remorse? Was he apologetic in some way to me? I agreed and signed.

In the court, we were almost next to each other, so I walked to the front bench to be away from him. I just didn't want to see him. The magistrate asked if I agreed and my intervention order was final – it was for a year. I didn't know how to react.

As I was getting ready to leave the courtroom, he was at the door. He opened the door for me, but I didn't budge. I waited for him to leave and so he did. Outside the court I ran to catch a last glimpse, but he was way ahead of me in the crowded street. I looked and looked, but I couldn't see him at all. Tears were forming in my eyes and I didn't know why. I should've been happy that I now knew how to take care of myself; I wouldn't be abused by him anymore. I still loved him, or was it me not letting go of all the abuse that I'd gotten used to?

I thought that was the last day I would see Amit, but the world is small and so is Melbourne. We crossed paths again in

September, exactly six months after the intervention order. According to the intervention order, he couldn't come any closer to me than five hundred meters, and in public places it was a gap of twenty meters or so. It was the city and a perfect scene of chaos. The mad rush of the lunch hour! I was travelling in that rush for a meeting in South Melbourne. Then I saw him! He was coming out from a nearby café. I wanted to change my path but I didn't. I was no longer afraid of him – he was just a stranger. We crossed each other and I gave him a scornful look.

But I didn't know that in a few weeks, I would be scorned again – and it would be the ultimate mutilation of trust and rape in the name of love, in the hands of Vamp Slayer.

***

How could I explain this to anyone? Perhaps I underestimated Ranju's strength, like I underestimated my own. She was being pushed into this foreign concept of arranged marriage; I never knew that I would be summoned to conquer her fears on marriage. The miracles of God will work on her in God's special way. Was it God's plan for me to believe in love again? Things were happening in front of my eyes, trying to tell me to let go of the past, to set myself free – but that could only happen if I made that choice.

CHOICES – JUNE 2011

> "I remain mistress of mine own self and mine own soul."
>
> —Tennyson

I always had choices in my life between right and wrong. I chose wrong with Amit because at that time, it seemed right to me. But if I hadn't made those choices, I wouldn't be able to understand that they weren't right for me – or appreciate what is good now.

It was 2011 and it had been a year and two months since I went into that courtroom in Melbourne to close a difficult chapter in my life. It was time to let go of the past and make peace with it. It wouldn't be right to say that only women are strong; humans are strong, and we don't know our strength until we're tested. We surrender ourselves to the situation and get ourselves entangled, making our lives as complicated as possible. Sometimes untangling a situation can also entangle us in the game of forgiveness.

Ranju and other women will have their own time; she will write her own history, good or bad. I was only advising her to make her own choices. Ranju and the other thousand Indian women were that same medium for me, summoned by God to reflect on myself, to make peace with my past, to forgive Amit and all the men in my life – and above all, to forgive myself and somehow believe in love again.

It was perhaps time to set the record straight. I kept my pen down and looked at the rays of sunlight seeping into my room through the window. I just smiled.

I was late today going to The Missing Peace. There was some kind of a meeting. Poonam was surrounded by the girls and she was telling them that she would be going to London to be with her daughter; we would have a replacement soon.

There were differences between her and the yoga instructor. I didn't know many details; all I could gather was that they were not getting along with each other. When the time came, Poonam asked me for her support. After all, I knew the yoga instructor through Poonam. She had all my support.

Poonam asked us to be in her studio next morning promptly, as she would be introducing us to her replacement. I was already missing Poonam.

***

The next morning, I cuddled the puppies outside the porch of our house and left for Missing Peace. Poonam was already there and as soon as she saw me, she grabbed me by the arm and took me to the back room.

'I have the tickets, I'm going to London. Oh, my clown, I'm so happy yet so nervous. How will I do it, leaving such responsibility on someone else's shoulders? I have to get everything in order here for the new teacher to take charge. The new girl is coming to teach today. I'm so nervous.' Poonam said, fretting and looking at me for some answers.

'It's going to be okay, I promise. Poonam, you have to go and be with your daughter. This place can look after itself, why do you worry so much? Sometimes you need to find your place to escape to and be with that particular thing that makes you happy.' I hugged Poonam.

Poonam looked exhausted and said, 'I know – the entire process of finding a yoga instructor is not only exhausting, but also it frustrates me to be treated so harshly. My husband bought the ticket last night and I was confused about what to do … I think I love this place so much that I forget myself, sometimes I forget what I want.'

I smiled; she made me realise that what we have in our lives, around us, is too hard to let go of – we get used to it. Sometimes to accept what we want is so easy, but we make it so hard for ourselves.

When the new girl arrived, Poonam announced, 'This is Apoorva, girls: she is a dancer and she'll be using some of her techniques in our classes.' Poonam asked all of us to greet Apoorva with the same enthusiasm we greeted her with each morning. Apoorva was in her early twenties and she was skinny as a stick but had the muscles of a dancer.

Over the next few days, things were getting hard for the girls at the Missing Peace, and for me. Apoorva tried her best to motivate us. 'Listen girls! I will tell you something funny. In the evening class, one of the girls … I dare not say her name … I asked her to improvise on her pelvic thrusts. She, on the contrary, didn't know what to say, and instead she said my pubic thrust is not good.'

I screamed laughing and it was quite a scream to shake up the quiet room. They didn't get the joke; only Jerry, Apoorva and I laughed. When Apoorva repeated herself, the room was shaking with quite a roar. One of the women was a doctor who sometimes could be very serious and she too couldn't stop laughing.

'What will we do when you're gone? Who would make us laugh? You certainly know how to include everyone in your laughter. It's not an easy task, you know,' she told me smiling. I didn't know if she saw the bruises I was hiding, or perhaps I was hiding them well enough from everyone. I was only human; I was laughing because it was funny. But I was indeed laughing after a long time from within. I was scared to laugh, as if I was adding a debt with a laugh and repaying it with my tears.

The next afternoon I was excited to get an email from Poonam that she had reached London safely; I was happy she remembered me far away from home.

***

The outside heat was staggering, and I was sheltered inside the air-conditioned room. I was thinking about my days in India. The people, the dust, the temples and, above all, the kindness I had been shown that I wouldn't have imagined. I let fear build in me because I was afraid to embrace their kindness. To me, any kindness shown to me always had shadows of doubts, but as a child and as a teenager, I would've always accepted it humbly, my heart filled with gratitude. I was fearless then.

My quest for love turned to kindness, trust and humanity. My journey is not new; it has been taken by millions of men and women across the planet in search of deliverance and repentance – but the ones who have the courage for repentance are the one who suffer the most. They suffer because they cannot withhold truths, keeping them secret. They try to hide them at certain points but their secrets catch up with them. I tried to hide them, allowing myself to find comfort in the arms of men – men who couldn't heal my wounds. Instead, one by one, they deepened the scars.

I never knew that to live, I'd have to go through such pain – and to laugh, I'd have to put a price on my life. Every laugh and every smile had a price tag. But then the life which gave me so much pain also gave me the strength to understand the meaning of new and old relationships. I looked closely at my relationship with the gods in their temples, my Maa and Baba, with the dogs and with the girls of Missing Peace – and, above all, Poonam. They all came with kindness, trust and belief.

I responded to everything, to be reborn again – but did I come all this way to India to find a broken chord? I did, in fact, find the fear that I was living with, the fear that tormented me every day to the point that I had to run away.

But life is not a hotel where we pack our bags and check in, only to find the nearest exit when there's an emergency. Neither can life be treated like a currency. When we cross borders from one country to another, money that was perfectly acceptable beforehand becomes worthless as soon as we cross that line. I was unsettled, so I changed countries and checked in here to identify my fears. If it were that simple, then we all would change countries because it takes a lot of courage to admit being wrong. Once we realise this, then the process of forgiveness becomes much clearer. Sometimes the miracles start and you begin filling the gaps, the missing pieces to the puzzle.

I wrote my history in Melbourne and it was time to make peace with the land that created my past and my present. I came all the way to India to find peace and forgiveness, but through that healing process I allowed myself to unlock my past – I had to come face to face with it again. It brought me closer to myself than ever before. It was time for me to go, to make peace with my past.

***

I saw a little girl running around the house, carefree and wild. I saw her hugging Maa and Baba and talking to them; I didn't quite hear what they were saying to each other but they were laughing. I'd never seen Maa and Baba so happy in their life.

'Maa who is she?' I asked. Maa didn't speak.

The little girl turned around to look at me – it was me, from when I was ten years old. She was smiling, not saying anything. She extended her hand to me; I was scared but then she gestured for me to come. As if in a trance, I took her little hand, so soft – I wasn't scared anymore.

We walked outside through the back door. I was still holding her hand. Outside there was a paddy field where I could see the ashram in front of me; on the left, I could see the temple of Bala jee, and on the right, Goddess Kali stood there in her temple.

My ten-year-old impression was now pulling me to run inside the paddy field, where I saw everyone standing. Where was I? Was it Vrindhavan or Jaipur? Suddenly, it didn't matter; the notion quickly faded away to the huge human chain that stood before me. They all formed a line, clapping and smiling as I entered the fields. I saw the girls of Missing Peace, and a faint frame of Sam typing away at a computer. I saw Amit, then Thomas, then Poonam. I saw my brother. I saw Issy, and my sister with my nephew and niece. I saw Ranju, carrying a baby in her arms. I saw Anthea and Sandy. I saw Khokhon and Jethu – and then I saw Maa and Baba. When I reached the end of the line, I saw the dogs and their puppies, wagging their tails and licking my feet. Then I saw me again, my ten-year-old version; I turned to my side but she wasn't there, she was in front of me instead. She reached for my hand again.

We walked further and I saw the burnt tail of the Qantas flight. I turned to her. She just smiled and slowly I could feel her hand slipping through mine. She was slowly fading into me. She nodded her head in approval and when I turned back to look, no one was there. It was an empty field and I was alone. I wasn't crying; I was calm and then I opened my eyes, sitting right up on my bed. I was scared, perspiring. I realised I was still in Delhi, in my bedroom. I must have fallen asleep while writing. I looked at my watch and it was six-thirty in the evening.

***

I was sitting in the travel agency waiting for the agent to come. He had given me a time for ten-thirty and now it was eleven-thirty. Jethu and I were waiting patiently for this agent to turn up; I was just about to pay another girl for the tickets when this man finally turned up. I paid for the tickets in a hurry and left.

Later that afternoon, I came back home to send Poonam an email that I had my tickets organised for Melbourne. I was about to shut down my laptop when I received an email from Vinod, the travel agent. The email read, 'Hope everything I've done was according to your needs, hope you have a comfortable flight and if there is anything you need, please kindly let me know. I apologise for keeping you waiting.' I replied to him it was okay. I think my Aussie charm was taking over the end of the email, like every other time I would write to someone, 'Thanks Mate!' It was my way of conveying thanks; unfortunately for him, I was a show-off from Australia.

He sent me another email saying that he was in Sydney a couple of years ago. So, the email conversation started to take action. I was getting a bit tired by now and asked him if he did any work or not. I thought that would put him in his place but it didn't; he openly asked me if I liked parties, if I liked to dance. I was surprised with his sudden wickedness and asked him if he was asking me out and what did he have in mind? To my surprise he was blunt enough to tell me that he was indeed asking me out. He added that he wanted to take a beautiful smile out to a beautiful dinner.

I laughed and replied that he was now flirting with me, before politely declining and switching off my laptop. I didn't want to mislead anyone before going back to Melbourne, partly because I wasn't ready for anything at all. I knew I could get carried away. The other part of me was saying, *what's the harm? It was just an invitation.* But I didn't know the guy, an absolute stranger doing my ticket. I was going back in three weeks.

I took a back step and let things be as they were, but I got a call from him to be advised that I was unfortunately not allowed to carry more than thirty kilos. 'So are we going out?' he added with an over-confident voice that annoyed me. I had to cut his confidence short with a professional tone. After I hung up, I felt a bit guilty – all he wanted was an answer to a question.

I was trying to be polite, and soon we were exchanging emails, talking about ourselves. I learned that he was divorced, had been working in Sydney and had to come back after his father passed away. He learnt that I was jobless, struggling to write my first book, and had no place to live after I went back to Melbourne. After all the formalities of getting to know each other were finally over, he made the same, quirky move. 'I think now you know me enough to go out?'

The persistent fool, I thought – how could I refuse? 'I would love just a cup of coffee, that's it. I think clubbing is not my scene and I'm living with my parents here, so it's a little difficult to go out at night.' He laughed at this statement but I didn't care. I had to respect Maa and Baba's values. I was living with them and surrounded by Indian middle-class values and eyes. I wasn't ready for any scandalous judgments, nor was I ready for my parents to get excited. Though nothing else mattered to me anymore, I had that pedigree of respect oozing through my veins.

The next few days, the text messages and phone calls started. We started talking and I came to know how young and submissive he was. He was telling me all about his life: how early he got married to his childhood sweetheart and how jealous she would get if she went out to dance with him. She ran away from home to get married to him and she ran away from him after a year of marriage, when he turned twenty-six.

Repeating his history, he didn't fret in asking me out. He was mentioning bizarre places such as a hookah place, and the new hangout for youngsters in shopping malls where you could pretend to smoke with the flavours of any fruit you could contemplate. Who was I kidding? I made it clear it was definitely not my thing.

***

At Poonam's, I was trying to enjoy my last few days with the girls. The yoga class moved out of Missing Peace and it was us girls versus the new dancing teacher, Apoorva. I told everyone that I would be leaving, three weeks from Poonam's arrival next week. I didn't realise that my news of going back would be received with such disappointment. I was rather sad too.

After every class, it had become a ritual for Jerry and me to gossip outside her house. I was fretting to tell Jerry about this sudden amusement in my life; when she heard about this, she laughed at my young boy's flirting. 'It doesn't matter what age they are, they're always horny in their own special ways. I'm thankful in every way that my husband and I ended up together, otherwise you know what it's like to work in hospitality. I always thought that he liked someone else from our group of friends but one day, as I was sitting behind his bike for a ride, I couldn't control myself and I burst into tears. He asked me why I was crying and I just told him that I loved him and couldn't bear the thought of him paying more attention to other girls rather than me. In saying that, he burst into laughter – actually, he was testing my patience as to when I would break down. He loved me and was waiting for me to say it. Nandita, don't read into it too much, go out for a coffee but don't be naive too. There is no harm in meeting him.'

I shook my head in approval. It had been eight months since my last testament in the name of love. It was just a coffee, but he had clubbing in his head and I wasn't sure what more delirious ideas he had. It could've been just an easy way to get laid, perhaps.

'Nandita, you're going away in a few weeks or so, and after that you won't see him. You don't know Delhi guys: they find any excuse for sex.' Jerry made an animated face.

'Were you reading my mind?' I said laughingly.

'I'll tell you something, just go and have some fun. You never know, yeah? He is young, don't expect so much,' she said, walking towards her house. Then she stopped to add, 'Be happy, Nandita – try to be.'

***

I looked at my watch: it was two-thirty. As I was sitting to type something to Poonam, the mobile rang and it was Vinod. 'So have you made up your mind?' I was impressed with his persistence. I thought about Jerry and thought I had to let go of the pretense; sooner or later I had to say yes, otherwise I was going to be hassled anyway.

We arranged for the next day. Knowing my parents' conservative views, I had to tell him to come and pick me up. I was scared of saying yes to him; I was suddenly nervous and thought to make an excuse, but I couldn't be chicken-hearted forever. I had to let go of fear and trust in myself again.

Now I had to speak to Maa. I couldn't believe that I had to seek permission to go out with a guy. Here I was, living with traditional parents, and here they were with their prodigal daughter. Why did I feel like this? I always had male friends coming to my house when I was living in Delhi before, but why hesitate now? Perhaps I was too conscious of what others might think or how they might interpret this out of context.

I was racing from one room to another, wondering how to break the news to Maa, and eventually I gathered the guts to just say it as blunt as possible. Maa was sitting at the dining table, peeling some potatoes. 'Maa, I need your permission, I want to … well! This travel agent, Vinod, who had done my tickets for Melbourne, has asked me to go out and have a coffee. Can I?'

Maa looked at me, gave a smile and then continued, 'Is he the one who's keeping you busy these days with phone calls?'

I was surprised I had a Miss Marple sitting in our own house – but then, nothing escaped a mother's eyes. We both laughed at this.

To my surprise, she not only took the news well but was very happy for me to go out – the same Maa who was usually too protective about me going anywhere. The only request she made to me was to go out during the day. 'You should introduce him to Baba, it's good to know someone who could help with cheap tickets and it's been a long time since you knew someone.'

I underestimated Maa. Then she said something that changed the whole idea of shame. 'How old is he?' I didn't know where this conversation was leading to, but I told her his age. 'Oh! Doesn't matter, that age gap is nothing … all you need is someone to marry you!'

I was shocked at this statement and I burst into laughter. 'Come on Maa, stop saying that ... he's just a friend who wants to go out for a coffee, what does marriage have to do with it?'

'He is young and you are not, so when a guy pesters you to go out, it means more than that.' Maa took her potatoes and walked away. She left me under eyes of judgment, like the *kaamwalis*. I was speechless; did I want to go now?

***

Vinod came to the door and the tension between us was apparent, so instead of a hug I just took him straight to the lounge. What was the appropriate way to greet someone? I introduced him to Maa and Baba and, quietly in a corner like a shy schoolboy, he ate the sweet that was offered to him. I was chatting away nonstop with everyone in the room, out of sheer nervousness and embarrassment. We rose to leave and Maa called me aside to tell me to be home by nine. I took a deep breath and said to her of course, without a doubt.

Once inside the car, Vinod showered me with his annoyance of the way I'd greeted him. It was a tease and I made it clear that he should've been more of a man to greet a woman. That cheered him, to my surprise.

We crossed the Delhi–Haryana border and were now in Gurgaon; it's primarily a hub for multinational companies, posh shopping arcades and hotels, as well as the homes of the very rich and wealthy.

He took me to a sports bar owned by an Australian; the lively jazz music was quite uplifting. I ordered a mocktail and he ordered a big jug of beer. 'Phew! I thought you would order a glass of wine that would cost me thousand rupees,' he joked.

I laughed. 'Don't worry, I'm not that heartless, I'll pay for my own drinks.' I winked at him.

We spoke about life and my book. He made a comment: 'Perhaps, I will be the end of your book.' It was the charm of a young boy who took every effort to impress a sheila like me.

I was looking at my watch as we talked more about his relationships; I was literally swept away by his charm. 'Let's go, otherwise your mother will think I've kidnapped her daughter.' I laughed.

Once in the car, like any other young Delhiite, he turned up the music player so loud – an attention seeker, every passer-by would have thought. I tried to tell him to keep it down, but he wouldn't listen. I wanted to get out in embarrassment, but it was so much fun that I found myself completely enamored with its beats. The scene reminded me of when I was eighteen in Delhi, though I was not a big fan of trance music – I was happy with my brother and our friends playing loud music that we all enjoyed. Times have changed, so have people, but I was in a car with Vinod, travelling through the passage of yesterday again.

He dropped me off at the back lane that led to the entrance of the house; my friend came wagging his tail, circling us. Vinod patted his head and I smiled at the scene, it was beautiful. Suddenly, the dog sat, as if he was waiting to watch what happened next – but I guess I disappointed my friend, since nothing happened. Vinod and I just hugged and parted ways, saying goodnight. I think that must have infuriated my little furry friend, as he started barking. He wanted to be an audience and clap for me, but instead I guess he must have said, 'What a waste of time.'

Maa was sitting in the lounge, relieved to see me. 'I called you so many times, I was getting worried you know,' Maa began to say.

I checked my phone and I saw ten missed calls. 'Sorry Maa, there was music so I couldn't hear,' I said to her with a hug, knowing I was meant to check my phone – but I was carried away by Vinod's charm.

'He seems like a nice boy. You never know, marriage is also something you would consider with him.'

I laughed at Maa's remark and was beginning to get the sinking feeling of Maa being misled again by this sudden chaos. 'Maa, he is just a friend – nothing to misinterpret, nothing is happening. I'm going away and there's nothing more important than that,' I said to her as calmly as possible.

'Well! You can change it by staying here and working things out.'

I didn't know what to say to Maa this time, but I was annoyed with her.

***

'Poonam, this is for you!' I gave Poonam a photograph of mine; below it I'd written a short poem about her and the Missing Peace. She was smiling. 'Poonam, thank you. I dedicate this to you, like you have dedicated this to me. I dedicate Missing Peace to you.'

Poonam was confused and gave me a questioning look. I smiled. She read the poem again:

> To the Missing Peace: I had been a lost world when I came knocking into the gates of Missing Peace. I chose to be scared, I chose to be frail.
>
> Suddenly, there was this beam of extraordinary strength. There were smiles around me, hope around me, faces of extraordinary courage. One by one, I tried to catch them for my missing puzzle.

Slowly the fatigue settles, the lips start to break into a smile and the soul begins its healing.

The mind starts to be free and the heart starts to somewhat feel again. I start to feel alive again and wished I could capture each of you in a *tabeez* (amulet) and wear it like a priceless gem protecting me from my insecurities ...

When the dust of the past obscures my eyes again, I could look back at the *tabeez* and smile again.

I love you all and I will miss you and your Missing Peace; through you and the girls, I have found that missing piece in that jigsaw puzzle we all call life.

Yours sincerely,

Your truly mad clown.

Poonam was almost in tears and so was I. 'Thank you, Poonam!' I said. 'You and the girls have helped me through a difficult stage of my life. Those little fragments of conversations may be nothing to you but to me they were priceless, they were everything. Your calling from London while watching *The Lion King*, as you were missing me and thinking about me ... it was like you were taking care of me all the way. The amazing women you gathered have showed me the way to love life and live it. You and the girls pulled me through my time here in India. I came here falling to pieces and feeling like there was no hope for me, but new relationships helped me to understand the long journey ahead. I couldn't have done it without you or the girls. You made me realise my own strength.'

At this point I was choked up. Poonam was just looking at me, her tears imminent.

Poonam hugged me and I let loose the tears. One by one the girls of The Missing Peace came into the room and, like two lovers, we had to break free from each other.

***

Over the next few days and weeks, I took some photos of the girls and decided to give everyone a token of me – and I kept a token for myself too. Each time I needed a piece of peace, I would look at them and treasure it forever. I was summoned by God to be here and the temples helped me open my eyes to see them. The red wristband from Bangla Sahib, given to me by one of the girls, was to conquer my fears; the conversation, good or bad, helped me to identify with what lay beneath the shadows of doubt. I would celebrate this going away, so the sorrows could depart and the old soul could be unified with the new.

***

That afternoon, I was sitting at Jerry's place after a beautiful lunch with Poonam and Astha. Jerry was asking about my date with Vinod. I mentioned the conversation, but then there was nothing more to mention. She was showing off her family album: photos of her and her husband when they met for the first time. There were beautiful photos of them in the living room and the bedroom, which I noticed when I followed her there to pick up her two-year-old son. She kept both her Anglo and Hindu culture in a fine balance by naming her two sons in that same fashion.

'What a nice photo, you look so very young,' I said to Jerry, pointing at that photo.

'Yes, I was in my early twenties. Someone said to me once that I shouldn't always keep photos of myself alone. It should always be with him so that way, love always grows. Photos of us always keep that togetherness.' I smiled at Jerry's simplicity and was very touched.

We were talking about life and so forth when my phone rang. It was Vinod. 'The last day is finally here. So, you gave me your word to spend the whole day with me tomorrow?' I replied without hesitation: yes.

'I never said that I'd go with him but now I have to,' I told Jerry afterwards. She was laughing.

Then Vinod texted me. 'Can't wait to spend the day with your arse.'

I laughed at this and so did Jerry. 'Man! He is into you,' Jerry said to me with a wink.

'He's twenty-four, Jerry, what was I doing when he was born?'

'Perhaps you were having your period?'

'Eek!' I laughed, but I was getting disappointed because I knew it would soon be over before it started.

***

Maa was trying to help me with the packing and I was telling her to leave it, as it could be done at night – I had nothing to pack and I could manage on my own. She felt a bit disappointed and Baba looked at me. 'Let her help you, she wants that bit of satisfaction.' I nodded and hugged both of them.

Astha called to tell me that she was in the lane, waiting to take me to The Missing Peace. I ran with twenty-three blown up shots of me and the girls, and a poem dedicated to every girl. Once in the car, Astha gave me an amazing hug; she was in tears. 'Here, this is for you.' I handed Astha the photo of the Missing

Peace and me. 'Whenever you miss me, you can look at me and read the poem, my dear. I know you're not in the photo – you had your exams that day – but you can still see me and I have you in my poems.' I smiled at her.

'Oh! Before I forget, I brought something for you too. It's not big but something that will remind you of me too.' Astha handed me a small pouch.

I opened the pouch and saw four beautiful silver oxidised bangles. 'It's beautiful … as beautiful as you!'

All the girls at The Missing Peace were as delighted as Astha; from the first girl to the last, they had the same delirious 'puppy' face as me. I hugged each and every one of them.

I walked out to sit in Astha's car. I turned to look back at the gates of The Missing Peace for the very last time; my eyes were overshadowed with tears. I didn't know when I would see it again and I didn't know how I would manage without them – but now I had the love, strength and courage of twenty-four women. Somewhere in their prayers I would be prayed for, somewhere in their tears I would be cried for and somewhere in their smiles I would be smiling. I would miss them indeed.

***

I went to the temple with Maa to say my final goodbye to Maa Kali. As I was walking up the temple, I saw her, exactly like the last time I saw her, sitting immaculately in her red sari under the chandelier. Today, she said nothing, just smirking at me.

I was the one who spoke today. I offered a silent prayer to her. 'Thank you for showing the path to where I belong. Through my dreams you have interpreted your miracle: through the girls of The Missing Peace, through Maa and Baba, through the dog's family and through me. I pray to you and hopefully this prayer of mine can be transmitted to the gods by you. I hope you can be my messenger today, as everyone in my life recently has been your miracle and messenger to me. I thank you for giving me those fears of the past so I could stand here and face those fears. Guide me on these rough roads, as I have a long journey ahead. I say goodbye to you here, but in my heart you're here forever. Through you, I have learned to ask the right things in my prayers. Through Guru jee, you have taught me to believe in the connection I'd forgotten. I thank you for teaching me how to believe in prayers and miracles again.'

I opened my eyes to look at her and those eyes were shining. Was it the light from the ceilings or the festal lights in the temple? Her tongue was still sticking out – this time though, she was not mocking me. In fact, they had the playfulness of a mother taunting her child, carrying the feeling that from here on, it was going to be smooth. I just had a malfunction that needed to be tuned.

I came home from the temple to see Ranju waiting for me with her girls. I hugged each one of them, as I knew they would part ways with Ranju one day. I gave Ranju a big hug and one of my photos, so she didn't forget me, and huge chocolates to remind her of the sweetness she added in my life with her courage.

***

'Vinod, where are we going?' I asked Vinod at the top of my voice, as it was too loud in the car with his music.

'Don't worry, I'm not hijacking you, I will let you fly on that plane,' he said mockingly. 'It's my day with you, so leave it to me.'

I smiled. 'Why not? Wherever you want me to go, I will go with you.'

We were circling the roads of South Delhi and then we were off to Gurgaon again. 'Let's watch a movie, what do you say?' I nodded and we ended up watching *The Hangover: Part Two*. I was with a young guy, so I had to respect his ideas of a perfect date.

After the movie, we were at the parking lot so I thought this was the right moment to give him a photo of me and a poem written for him – something that would remind him of me. He looked at the photo and left it on the dashboard. He didn't read the poem or say anything, as if he was not interested at all – the same Vinod who, a few weeks ago, was so fascinated about books. It was imminent; I was slowly fading away in his memories.

We continued talking about my book, though I think he had nothing to say to me, nor was there anything left in his magic bag of words. He said once again that he would be the ending to my book. I just took a deep breath and I managed a frown at him, asking him to start up the car for a drive.

He halted the car next to a bottle shop and asked me what I would fancy. I didn't drink beer like him, so I was happy with vodka. I must have drunk two Bacardi Breezers and already felt tipsy – his continuous smoking made it worse. I was well and truly drunk with the third bottle. Whether it was the weather outside, the music in the car or the charm of a young boy, I was feeling very flirtatious and suddenly I wasn't me. I felt like a sixteen-year-old who'd just finished her day at school, rejoicing the start of summer holidays.

I felt young, like my early days in Delhi. It was an unbelievable experience, as if I was reborn again in that lost time. If alcohol could play such tricks then I would be drinking every day to revisit my past. I knew each sip I took subdued the pain of being wanted again, but I never knew it could give me a flashback. I dare say it was nostalgic.

But, I never did get into the loitering ways like today, with a young boy beside me. Never in my school or college days would I have dared such philandering.

The roads of Delhi were transformed, like me, from the relics of its own façade. The dust of history was apparent on Delhi's road and on my face. For a brief moment, my hands brushed with Vinod's when he changed the gears of the car. There was this tingling sensation on my hand; I forgot what it felt like. Was it the alcohol that was raising this dubious passion in me?

I slowly brought my lips next to his ears and planted a soft kiss on his cheek – and the next thing I knew, I was nibbling his ears and kissing his face. Slowly he responded to my sudden act of infatuation; he was as speechless as my drunken self, but I let go of any morality. It was Delhi – it was me and it was my time.

I had no care in the world about the other cars passing by; I had no shame. How could I? I was consumed with the old dust of New Delhi. I was reintroducing myself to the commotion of the New Delhi that I'd left behind.

I'd never kissed a boy on the roads of Delhi before. Was I judging myself? I was walking in the shadows of my past – was I starting all over again? I scolded myself; it was my time.

Vinod had to break free from me as he stopped at a red light, but nothing stopped me; I took one of his fingers slowly in my mouth, caressing and kissing it. One by one, I sucked his fingers as if I was suckling on a honeycomb, appreciating the sweet nectar that it offered to me.

He was defenseless; he had to stop the car before I could take control. He pulled me closer and I grabbed his hair as we finally kissed. We were unstoppable, his hands all over my body. But then the mobile rang. I had to come back to my senses. I gave a soft push to Vinod to free myself from this illicit passion. I didn't want to give up but I had to – it was already time.

'Where are you? Come and spend a few hours with us too,' Maa said very affectionately.

I replied to her that I would be home very soon. I tried to make myself presentable again and brushed my hair. I checked myself in the mirror and I was in horror: my lips were swollen, as if I was stung by a bee. I looked like a different person altogether, my own reflection mocking me.

I put the mirror down and looked at Vinod; he wasn't smiling. He looked at me, not a care in the world for my swollen lips; instead he put his left hand around my shoulder and his right hand on the steering wheel. 'Don't look at me like this, I will fall in love with you.' Vinod said that with such conviction, it was hard to ignore. He pulled me towards him again and this time I was quiet, scared of what he just said. I was nervous; I just lay my head on his shoulder and closed my eyes.

I wanted to lighten the mood, break this silence and hide my thoughts from him. 'You don't want to look at your own painting? You know, you can't hide now; you have left your masterpiece on my lips. I shall have to carry this now to Melbourne. It will be on display.'

He laughed at this joke but was still sombre. How would I explain this to Maa and Baba? I was carrying his burden on my lips for the entire world to mock me once again. It was just a twisted tale of a boy meeting a woman, a human error in the name of passion that we sometimes confuse with love.

Vinod left me in front of my house and I didn't hug him or say anything – I just touched his face and walked, not looking back. I knew he was standing there for a long time, waiting for me to look back at him, but I didn't. I was sad but I didn't want him to see what I was feeling. I didn't want his sympathy. Tears were building up in my eyes, but I didn't let them betray me today, I wasn't going to cry for this.

***

'What happened to your lips?' Maa asked me curiously.

I looked away and said, 'I had prawns for lunch and you know, sometimes they give me an allergic reaction.'

Maa was trying all sorts of medications on me and I had the mixed concoction of guilt and nervousness. Why is it so easy to hide one lie and equally difficult to cover the other? And so I had everything that she offered me. 'Just before you go, you had to have prawns … wasn't there any other dish available?' Maa said, folding my clothes and handing them over to me to place in the suitcase. Baba joined Maa in alliance to show some discomfort in me having prawns.

But, what could I have had? That was the only dish in front of me and I paid the price for my greed, being bitten by an angry or hungry prawn.

I stood there for a long time, looking at myself in the mirror; suddenly I saw I had no earring and then had a momentary flashback of Vinod and me in the car. I knew it was doomed. I saw her staring back at me, my ten-year-old impression laughing at me. I looked away and then looked back again to see if it was real. There was no one; it was just me, staring at myself in my present. Who is this woman? All I could do was just smirk at the new me.

THE ACCIDENT – NOVEMBER 2011

> "I tried to drown my sorrows, but the damn things learned how to swim."
>
> –Frida Kahlo

When death silently knocks at one's door, one feels the urge to live. The mind orders the body to live. The volatile heart finally weeps. The body needed its final journey to rest, but it's just a carcass of bones and veins. How can death be victorious? Is it the body or is it the soul it's after?

I was scared, petrified and then suddenly I saw her – I saw my Dida. She wore her white sari in the same fashion that she used to in Delhi. Her skin was clear of the eczema.

She extended her hand to me. I tried my best to reach out to her but then I heard someone calling my name: 'Nandita, can you hear me? Can you hear me, sweetheart? You are at the Alfred Hospital! You have fractured your skull … do you have a contact nu …' The voice faded away and so did my Dida, her beautiful kind face slowly vanishing in the corner. Closing my eyes, I fell into a deep sleep until I woke up to a familiar voice: 'I am here!'

It was my sister. I tried to open my eyes to see her, to understand what was happening, but I couldn't. My head was heavy and my body was numb. I tried to move or open my eyes again, but slowly I refrained from trying as if it didn't matter anymore. I needed to sleep and never wake up.

I finally started to understand what was actually happening. I was lying in a hospital bed, trying to move my head but my neck was strapped with a collar. I was at least comfortable in my own discomfort. Spacing in and out of sleep or consciousness, it didn't matter. I was trying to put the pieces back into this puzzle. The bloodstained pillow where I rested my bandaged head was indicative of this. I closed my eyes. The hospital noise faded into the background.

***

It was a Saturday when Harry, Bianca (Harry's sister), Helen (one of Harry's rowing camaraderie) and I all went for rock climbing to Mt Cathedral; we camped the previous night and set out the next day for climbing.

The trail was difficult to start with, but we soon found the perfect cliff to climb. Bianca was at her best, fit as a fiddle. She was unstoppable and climbing the hill like a wild cat without any ropes or harness. She was used to it and practice made it perfect. She and Harry went to the top of the hill to fasten the ropes while Helen and I sat on a boulder, chatting away. It was a hot day and we reminded ourselves every moment to keep hydrated.

Once Harry had his ropes prepared, Helen went up first; her determination to climb the rock was very inspirational for a novice like me. She had a few problems with abseiling but once she got it right, it was a smooth ride home. Then it was my turn.

It was very hard to start with, but the others were patient with me until I climbed to the very top. As if this was the climb of a lifetime. I was barefoot and each boulder had a repetitive, difficult feel to it – the ruggedness of the cliff was brutal. I somehow made it to the top and felt as if I had successfully climbed Mt Everest.

I'd never done this before; to climb that hill was an enormous achievement. I always got excited whenever I saw the sport on TV with Harry, and would always get inspired with the climbing fanatics, but to see and try were two different things. I was always living on the edge; taking one risk after another didn't scare me one bit, even though it was challenging. Perhaps that kept me motivated.

I was relieved to see Harry still holding me with the rope. It was my turn to abseil. I tried over and over to fall back but my nerves got the better of me; I challenged myself but I couldn't do it anymore. I was worried that if I failed to abseil, Harry would end up falling with my weight attached to the rope. I gave up, forgetting I was still attached with a rope and I still had my harness on.

Bianca came to the top of the hill where I was standing, and I don't know what overcame me – I detached the rope and took off my harness. Bianca was showing me the easy route to cross over the other side of the hill. All I had to do was follow her instructions carefully.

To cross, I needed to leap to a solid rock and rest my foot on the other landing; there was a gap in between the two. It was difficult as my legs were not long enough to stretch out. I tried with a final push but one of my legs slipped.

I just remembered falling and praying – 'God please don't make me an invalid' – and the rest was history.

Now, in that hospital bed, I felt the coldness of life for the first time – the brutality of being alone and written off as a victim was terrifying. No one was there: just me, myself and this huge space of hospital coldness. All I could do was stare at the ceiling blankly. I lifted my hands to see if I was really alive and then I noticed, on my right hand, the tattoo of a phoenix. Franklin! I drifted again.

***

In the week following the night Franklin dropped me outside the flat, I lost my job at the company. It was God's miracle that I bumped into him the very afternoon I was shown the door. He walked me home and we took a detour for a coffee. We talked, laughed and spoke about our lives again. 'I don't know what to do; I have my ex on the side and then Sweets.'

We held hands and I said to him again, 'Be brave.' He was trying to encourage me by saying that what I lost was just a job that I didn't enjoy doing anyways, and it wasn't an end to anything. We were reminding each other of our strengths and weaknesses.

Nothing mattered to me in that moment – just me being with him and listening to his voice. It didn't matter I'd just lost a mere job. I woke up in the morning feeling happy, wishing Baba a happy birthday, and now I was sitting here with Franklin, drowning the happiness of the day in a cup of hot chocolate. Nothing else mattered. Once near home, I asked Franklin, 'Can you do me a favour?'

'Yes?' He was walking beside me and I paused for a while.

I said, 'Just stay in my life.' I'd now submitted to my fears of what just happened: I'd lost a job and the daunting feeling of losing Franklin was imminent.

We hugged each other goodbye. That was it. I never saw him again nor did I hear from him again. A few texts here and there and after a while, that stopped too. I saw the phoenix engraved in my hand as a testimony of him. It was a gift to me for my thirty-sixth birthday, something that would remain with me forever. Money can buy perfumes or a good dinner, but not those few moments that I had spent with Franklin- they were priceless and I had to pay a tribute to him.

I knew it was not the end; there were still so many things left to say to each other, and many coffees to share. I didn't have his number anymore but it was better left this way, for nature to take its course on life. Perhaps we would cross paths again and perhaps he would remember me.

Those weeks after losing the job and Franklin were like days of mourning. I wasn't so sad from losing the job as I was for losing him. I didn't know much about him, but it was as if I knew him all along. There were many distractions in the middle, but I wasn't distracted. I didn't reciprocate any infatuations. Was it again a healing process?

That job was just a medium for us to meet – and then when we finally met, it was time for us to go. Was it a miracle or a belief that I had kept him alive in my mind, to live with for the rest of my life? Did I just like him as an idea, or was it beyond explanation?

Those months were difficult; the only allowance was Andrea Bocelli's 'Caruso' to forget him, but that too couldn't free me – my eyes were dry, tired of tears. However, there was still this last tear hiding somewhere within me, as if I was saving it. The song is about a dying man in pain and longing, who looks into the eyes of the girl who was very dear to him.

My mind was back in the hospital. I touched the tattoo with my fingers still covered with the dust of the mountains. My eyes were drowsy from the drugs and the pain in my head forced me to drift into a semi-conscious state; once again I was failing myself.

***

No water or food, as the doctors were waiting to operate on my head. It didn't matter to me anymore. They were waiting for some sort of black hole in my head to close, caused by the fracture. If it didn't close, they had to operate. I would be told this by the nurse every time I would scream for water.

My legs were tied with some kind of compression for the circulation of blood; I couldn't move my body or my head because of the collar. The only way to move was when two nurses came at night to massage some cream on my back. One would count, 'One, two and three,' and then both of them turned me from one side to another. That was the only time I could feel rested.

The only time I was given a drink was an ice cube to suck. I remember screaming at a male nurse, complaining about the pain in my head, and the torture of my collar. I would continue pressing the bell, and then slowly the anger would fade away until I woke up in the morning. I didn't want anything, just water. I said sorry to him, and after that I stopped complaining.

What was I complaining about? I didn't need water, only my body needed it – the soul was free of a burden to live. Soon the desire of having water was also lost. I didn't want anything anymore. Pain was familiar to me, so what was this pain I was complaining about? All hope had been snatched away. I gave up!

It didn't make any sense, considering the prayer I made to God not to make me invalid. I was already an invalid in the eyes of others.

***

'What date is it? Where are you?' the nurse was asking, while I was heavily sedated.

'I don't know.' I had my eyes closed. I remembered I went for climbing on a Saturday so it must be the 6th. (I was wrong –

it was the 7th). I dozed off again, but then something about Maa and Baba forced me to open my eyes. I tried to close my eyes and not see their flashes in front of me, but I opened my eyes again and they still haunted me.

Just a week before the accident, Maa and Baba were leaving for Delhi after their three-week visit to Melbourne. They were living with my sister and her in-laws. I thought it was a perfect chance to mediate between my brother, my sister and my parents.

I contacted my brother on my return from Delhi to connect the broken bloodline, but that connection was excruciating. I was begging and I was thrown a penny: I was accepted to see a glimpse of my niece in the flesh, whom I hadn't seen since her birth. 'Please let me meet you all. Let's reconcile, I don't have much time.' We were both guilty parties, but Delhi gave me a chance to sneak into my past and forgive all that was there to forgive, including with him and myself.

I tried the best I could to reconcile between him, Maa and Baba, but I didn't realise that the simple process would lead to a family war. Everyone shut me out of their lives – or was it me shutting everyone from their lives? Why did the reconciliation process have to be a war of egos and fury – why did it always have to end with me paying a price?

Baba and Maa left; Baba didn't say one word of goodbye to me. The gap between my sister and me was stretched out so far that my voice couldn't even echo across the gulf between us.

I tried to lose myself in the new job but that didn't help. The night before leaving for camp, I locked myself in my room and cried. Everyone in my life, one after one, all left me with these unanswered questions. Are human emotions so brittle that they cannot face love? Is ego superior to bloodline? It doesn't matter who's right, who's wrong – what matters is the person who wants a truce. Everyone blamed me for being wrong; I did what I thought was right. But if I was wrong, then who was right?

In that little chase of peace and war, everyone chased me away. I was alone once again.

***

'I can still cancel your ticket, just tell me.'

'I can't, Vinod! I just can't. Let's talk about something else. I will give you my number once I get myself organised in Melbourne again.'

There was silence on the other side of the phone. Vinod just said that he would meet me at the airport, and he hung up.

The next morning, Maa and Baba were sad but I motivated them to be happy. I was looking forward to returning to Melbourne.

I was waiting with Maa and Baba for Vinod to come to the airport before I checked in. Out of nowhere, Maa said to me, 'He is not that bad, no one is perfect.'

'Maa!' I frowned at her. The conversation was cut short when Vinod came from behind. He greeted Maa with the Indian custom of touching the feet of the elders. I was okay with it; in Delhi that was expected of any normal guy in India. I didn't dare kiss him but, foolishly, I washed myself with the shame of Delhi's dust one last time. I whispered closely on his ears, 'Look at the allergy of prawns on my lips.'

'I didn't tell you to have them, did I? But you can if it pleases you so much.'

I burst into a little giggle. I looked to my left and to my right if anyone was watching us. I had to be careful as public affection was still not accepted – but what would they do, arrest me? I was leaving anyway. So I planted a soft kiss on his mouth and turned back to see if Maa and Baba saw me. To my relief they didn't.

I was making my way to the gates when Vinod pulled me softly closer to his ears and whispered, 'I will miss you.'

'Then miss me,' I said to him.

He began to say something but paused. He touched my cheeks. 'I have your earrings that must have fallen …'

'Keep them. When you think about me and me only, you can fall back on those earrings.'

On the flight, I knew this was the last time I would see him. Over the first days back in Melbourne, I not only felt the cold chill of the Melbourne weather but also the coldness of Vinod's affection. I gave him my number, but the phone calls got reduced to chats on the laptop, and then emails. Then there was nothing except a final blow to my short-lived infatuation. He would gossip about his flirtatious ways with other women and try to fish for any kind of bitterness in me. I would be sad but not angry. One day I just talked about us; it was good I did, and it would have been better if I didn't.

'You make me sad and we are friends, so what's this rush about us? I asked you to stay – you didn't. So perhaps it's good you are gone, with me here. You have to find a job, a place to stay and get on with your life. I need the space to think about what I want. I thought you were intelligent enough to know.'

'Come on, we are friends and no friends can make each other sad. I was, you know, just curious after all …' I paused for a while. 'Please, just one request: as friends are not supposed to make each other sad, I ask the same from you for me too. I need you to be mature enough to understand that I didn't have to know of any of your philandering with other women to make me go away. You could have just asked.'

I was very polite and said goodbye to him – I was bidding farewell to our infatuation that night. I guess he understood that and he apologised for his behaviour. The dust of Delhi finally rubbed off my face and left shame on me forever. Selfishness can never cover up the truth; it always brings up the true personality and character of a person. Truth is a brutal thing when one cannot face it; it hides within guilt, pretending and lecturing on morality. I was not in love with him; I was enamoured by him. I just had the idea of love.

***

I tried to open my eyes and all I could see was a faint blue necklace; I closed my eyes only to be woken up by my sister's voice. She was talking to the nurse; I couldn't understand any of it and I slowly drifted back to sleep.

When I woke up, I saw a team of doctors in front of me … was it the same day? I'd lost count. 'Remove the urinal and the collar and she can have something to eat,' one of the doctors advised the nurse.

I looked away and then the nurse asked me if I would like to eat anything. 'Waa … water please.' The nurse erected the bed into a sitting position. I didn't want to get up; I tried to turn my heavy head, but I still couldn't, even without the collar.

'Come on, try to get up slowly and have this water.'

I looked at the nurse and I didn't move. I was comfortable like this; I found a place to rest and I wasn't giving it up, not even for a cup of water. The thirst has been quenched, just like the burden that I had been carrying on everyone's behalf. My head rested on the serenity of the hospital pillow. It was indeed the final journey for the body to make peace with the soul. I couldn't give up this surreal peace for starting all over again. Could I?

***

'Come on, you need to eat now.' I was quiet and looked at my sister for a long time. She hadn't been speaking to me since Maa and Baba had left Melbourne. Why was she here? I was angry. I didn't want to give up my silence and make a truce. 'How did you come to know about me?'

She set down the food and sat close to me. 'You gave my number?'

I was puzzled for a while – how on earth did I manage to do that? Then I remembered seeing Dida, and the nurse was asking me for a contact number. At that moment it seemed that I still did have the hope to live – and after all, blood is thicker than water.

'You're very lucky to be alive, that's what the doctors kept repeating when they brought you here. I got a call from the hospital around nine at night. I put the children to bed and left them with the sister-in-law. When I came, they made me sit with a glass of water. You know what I asked them? "Is she alive?"'

I turned away from her and closed my eyes. There was again the rise of that last and final tear that I was hiding until I saw the tattoo. I was hiding it from myself and from everyone. I was very weak indeed to not confront my own guilt of abandoning everyone.

I ate a spoonful of the soup that Sumita was feeding me. I realised that even at the crossroads of life and death, I didn't give up on myself or on the bloodline that was disconnected.

***

'Mashi, look at your eyes, it's as if you've been boxed by someone,' my six-year-old niece Diya said to me. I tried to raise my hand to touch her cheeks but her *mashi* (aunty) was too weak to reach her.

'I told you, Mashi, that tattoo is a bad luck for you,' said my then nine-year-old nephew, Yash.

'Maybe that tattoo saved Mashi.' Politely telling off Yash, my sister just smiled at him.

I looked at the tattoo again; maybe she was right. Maybe I was that sacred bird that had risen from the dead. All along, I'd failed to see what Franklin had seen on the first day we met – it was as if he was trying to tell me this day would come. I am indeed the phoenix tattooed in my own arm. It occurred to me it was Franklin all along, the messenger from the universe, who presented me with a gift and picked up the pieces of this day. The day had come to rise from the ashes again. He saw me more clearly than anyone ever before. For the first time in days I smiled.

***

'Come on Nandita, get up … you have to walk, otherwise we will keep you here forever.' I looked at the nurse who was trying to be very polite and at the same time, like a matron in a hostel – she was not asking but ordering. I was convinced I was the sacred bird risen from the dead, and I needed to make the new journey.

I tried to get up to walk to the bathroom; my head was spinning, but I managed. I kept looking at the tattoo till I could reach the door at the end of the ward, reaching for the iron rod of the bed for balance.

The nurse grabbed me and rested me on the bed. 'Lay down for a while and then I'll take you to the bathroom for you to open up your bowels, then a nice warm shower.'

I entered the bathroom and I came face to face with myself for the first time in days. I saw the bruises on my face. Now it made sense what Yash, my nephew, was on about. My face was swollen, and my left eye had a heavy blood clot. Under my right eye, I saw a huge purple bruise. My cheeks were covered with cuts and bruises. My arms had the same bruises and my right leg suffered the most because of the fall.

***

I was packing all the summer clothes in one suitcase to keep in the garage of my sister's house, so that there was some room to walk around the study and for the kids to play. It felt as if I was overcrowding the house with my clutter. The tiny study (which was my room) was filled with books, toys, a computer – and me and my suitcases.

I was just about to open the door to take the suitcase out when my hand got caught in the bag and there was a huge thud. My entire portfolio bag was on the carpet and with it came out all the papers, pens and notebook. I was sorting the papers and then I came face to face with the intervention order – flashes of Amit and I followed. Ever since I'd come back from Delhi, I'd wanted to call him and speak to him, like I'd wanted to talk to Frank.

I tried Frank's number, but I couldn't reach him, as it was disconnected. I wanted to contact Amit, but it was hard for me to see him. I'd toyed with the idea but had to put it off until the next day and then the next week – until today, when I stumbled across the court order. It was indeed time to set the record straight.

I didn't have his number; I had deleted every little memory of him as I was moving from South Yarra to my sister's place before going to Delhi. I asked my sister if she had Amit's number and she was hesitant for a while. 'What's the use? Don't dig up old graves, it only brings the dead alive.'

'It's not that I want to start a relationship with him. It's something that I want for myself. It's time to make peace with him.'

My sister just left the mobile on the sofa and walked away.

'Hello!' His voice ran a chill over my spine, I hung up. Ten minutes later, I got a call on my mobile. 'I received a call on my mobile from this number, sorry who is this?'

There was no turning back now: I'd answered Amit's call. I guess it was time.

We decided to meet for lunch at his place. I was nervous, as this could open a whole new can of worms – but it was my own doing and there was no escape.

He was waiting for me outside the train station. He was the same person physically as when I left him. He commented on my hair, which was outgrowing the bob but still short. We talked and I learned that after the court hearing, one by one all the women in his life left him too. Lovers or friends, I didn't bother to ask. I told him about my trip to India and that I was writing a book. He was very happy; I didn't know why. I learnt he was supposed to get married but that didn't happen.

We were having lunch and talking, sitting very close to each other. I put my plate on the coffee table, turning to him; I slowly gave him a soft kiss on his cheeks and hugged him. I said to him I was sorry that things turned out so sour between us. 'Perhaps a little bit of honesty from your side would've saved both of us and we still could've been friends. I come to you today just as a friend, nothing more than that.'

'There were some faults in me too – I shouldn't have gone back to you, to and fro, when I was involved already. I shouldn't have treated you the way I did. I'm sorry. I don't know what engulfed me every time I saw you.'

Sorry: a simple word, but it has so much depth of repentance that an act of forgiveness becomes much easier than playing the part of a victim. He was wiping away my tears; he did have a heart after all.

It wouldn't be right to say that he lured me into getting intimate with him again; I was partly to blame too. He was showing me around his house and we walked into his bedroom. He opened his cupboard, showing me an expensive jacket he'd recently bought and then a pink shirt that I'd gifted him. I smiled; he really loved himself too much.

Was he trapping me in some kind of game? Maybe it was a mistake to come inside the bedroom. I was handling myself pretty well until he grabbed me for a kiss. The past was engulfing my present and slowly shackling me. Was I once again beginning a dangerous game? I didn't stop him though.

He was a different man today, and I a different woman. For the first time in these last three years, he'd finally learnt to say sorry and he was brave enough to admit he was wrong while looking into the eyes of his victim. I was a different woman because I didn't love him.

His kisses, his hands over my body, felt like nothing to me. His hands on each part of my body were as if he was releasing a prisoner from his cell. His love bites on my neck didn't even inflict the pain of love anymore. A dog can never straighten its tail and Amit could never be the man he wanted to be.

I quietly let him do what he wanted. I didn't feel any remorse or guilt. It wasn't the ideal way I wanted to make peace with him, but sometimes in the hands of fate we're all weak. It was like me giving him the final parting gift – *the gift of infidelity*. I say this because he cheated me with a woman and I am cheating him with my happiness.

I was amused with the sudden turn of fate. How the tables have turned today; he was begging me to stay and I was telling him I had to go. He was lonely.

I took a shower and was packing my bags when he offered me a glass of juice. I sat on his sofa, watching him. 'I told you I was supposed to get married,' he said. 'You know who she was?'

I was quiet for a while. 'Was it the same girl you cheated on me with?'

'She knew everything about you. We got engaged and she came here to stay with me until we planned to get married. She had no one, her parents had passed away.' He paused. 'I think she got cold feet and left me, saying she couldn't get married to me. She couldn't do this anymore.' To say anything after what he'd said wouldn't have been appropriate. But I burst into laughter, so hard that he was shocked at this inappropriate behaviour of mine. He hung his head in shame.

It would be wrong to say miracles had to play any part of this. I wasn't looking for any miracles; it was karma that had finally caught up with him. I wanted to be sad for him, but I couldn't bring up a word of sympathy. I just couldn't stop laughing.

Once in the car I was thinking, was it his ways that made her leave Amit, or was it that Amit could never love anyone but himself? When would he forgive himself?

That night I sent him a text. 'Sometimes we have to travel into our past to forgive our past, and in that process, we forgive ourselves too. I've forgiven you Amit, and hope you forgive me in some way too and free me from this burden. Release me.'

In the coming days, we were texting about general things. I felt the stab of yesterday in my heart. I was longing to see him, but I had to be strong. He left me an open invitation for a night-time rendezvous. He was indeed a strange man to understand.

In the following days, I was speaking to Maa on the phone and I learnt that one of the puppies, the little white one, was crushed to death under a car. I was sad and disheartened from losing a friend; I cried all night. The death of the little puppy may be insignificant to many, as he was just a stray dog, but to me he was one of God's miracles. I was like the dog's family, aimlessly walking without any direction. They embraced me and allowed me to believe that sometimes, new relationships are based upon glimpses of the old ones, which have the same feelings of humanity and kindness.

That was my time to be introduced to the dog family; now it felt as if the departed had bid its last farewell to me. I cried today, not for a human but for a puppy that couldn't speak, just feel and breathe. He was at peace now. I would miss a dear friend.

The next morning, I was in the bus on my way to work, still sombre with the news from the previous night. I was typing a text. 'Dear Amit, hope you are doing fine. I'm just writing to tell you that I'm happy you are back in my life, but I cannot offer anything more than friendship from here on. I'm happy to be just your friend. We can talk and I will definitely like you staying in my life but in a way a friend does, just not for benefits. I don't want to confuse each other as "we" again. I will definitely keep in touch and hopefully you will too.'

After that text message, I never heard from Amit – it said a lot about him as a man once again. I tried to say hello here and there but there was no response.

I always gave him news of what was happening in my life, including the move and losing my job. It was important for me to do that because a friend always keeps in touch with a friend. There was still no response; I knew I was fooling myself with the idea of being friends with him. He made his choice.

Just a month before the accident, I was coming out of the gym and found myself face to face with him again. He looked at me and I looked at him. I didn't want to say anything. When I came back to my flat, I told Harry that he called my name and I ran away but that didn't happen. He just looked at me and smiled. I didn't smile back, I just walked away. I made my choice.

***

The nurse held the hand shower to my head to wash my hair. I didn't move. I was weak, not from the physical strain but from thinking about the choices I'd made in life. The water was slowly washing away the dirt of the mountains and in a way, it seemed it was washing away my old life. The tears mixed with guilt and pain were slowly mixing with the water of the hospital. It was as if everyone was playing their sovereign part, not only recovering a woman from an accident but trying to recover her old soul.

I was changing into the white hospital robe, but I was reluctant to consider it pure. But I'd just had the holy bath and let myself believe that the clothes I'd been in when admitted to the hospital were stained with dirt, just like the clothes of my karma were stained with guilt, shame and pain.

They were discarded in exchange for a new white robe that was given to every patient to wear in the hospital. The simple robe was as colourless as karma and as pure and bright as the colour white. My karma had the stains because I was letting it have the dirt and not seeing beyond what is pure.

***

I was lying down when Harry and Brea arrived. 'Oh, wow, you're awake today!'

'Hi guys.' I tried to move myself slowly upright. 'I'm not only awake, I had a shower too.'

We had a quick laugh about both of us falling on the same day at the same time. The thing was that there were two groups.

'How's Helen?'

'She's fine. She came the other day, but you weren't conscious. I have to tell you this: after you fell, you had your head on Helen's lap and we took turns as your head had to be still, so it was kind of funny. Every time in your semi-conscious state you would tell her my head hurts and she would repeat, "I know".' We all laughed at this.

I knew what Harry was trying to do and I was deeply grateful to him for making me laugh. Brea gave me a big hug. I was thankful to be surrounded by such lovely and caring people. There is a saying: the people who stand by you in your bad days are the friends who remain forever.

***

'You lost a lot of blood, is there any kind of anaemic history in your family?'

'You mean hereditary? I don't think so, why?' I asked the doctor.

'We have to give you some platelets and a blood transfusion.' The doctor smiled and left with his team of doctors; on his way out, he advised something to the nurse.

So I received the transfusion. I asked the nurse what this yellow, orangey thing was, and she said, 'It's one unit of PRBC and one pool of platelets. It's good for you.' Later she said, in simple terms, it was packed red blood cells.

Suddenly, I remembered the truck that used to go past my flat, and on the back of the truck written in bold letters: 'Give blood, blood gives!' I was smiling, looking at the blood going into my veins. I closed my eyes, wondering if it would transform me into the person whose blood it had been. Would I be saved from the old me, or was it some kind of rebirth? The gift of God was a body with a soul; I did my best to look after the body, but in that rush, I forgot about my soul. Delhi gave me insight in trying to make peace with my soul, but I hadn't seen it until today: the price I had to pay to set it free.

If it was the new blood that has been travelling into every part of my body, touching every organ, then it had pumped out the old blood in my heart, making way for the new. The universe had already bestowed me with my identity; it was just a simple rebirth, being extracted from my own fears. They say the soul never dies but it does, so that it can be born again to reunite with the body and feel again. On the 5th of November 2011, when I fell from Mt Cathedral, I was born again.

***

'So what have you decided, Nandita?'

'Is there a way that I can go to rehab as an outpatient? I want to be with my sister for now,' I said to the doctor.

'Rehab is good for you.'

'I know it will be good for me, but I want to take these few days in transition.'

'Sometimes family cannot make that progress for you and every little thing you do is an achievement. Hmm. Very well then, if that's what you want, then we'll make all arrangements for you as an outpatient.' The doctor smiled and left.

***

I wanted to rest and unite with the love that had been hovering around me ever since my rebirth. So how could I let go? I promised the doctors I wouldn't miss any appointments and I would look after myself until rehab started.

The hospital is one of the most surreal places on the planet. It is chaotic with patients, families, doctors and nurses running around to save lives. The tears, the screams, the noise of the footsteps in the corridor and then the absolute silence of the night.

It's one of the most daunting places to come face to face with fear, which we often forget to look beyond. Using those fears wisely is being wise. We would never know how to transform ourselves if we didn't have fears. Everyone in that hospital had fears: the patients feared death, their families feared they would never see their loved ones again and the doctors feared they wouldn't deliver any miracles. For the first time, I began to appreciate having fears. Fear is beautiful; it is the road to courage and redemption.

***

'Radhe! Radhe! Guru jee, please accept my *pranam* ('Namaste' with folded hands).'

'Bless you my child, are you enjoying your new birth? This rebirth is a new gift for you; spend your new life wisely.' I was speaking to Guru jee on the mobile to seek his blessings. In fact, he just confirmed that my new birth was imminent. It was the only truth that I had to accept – the rest was sublime.

***

I was waiting outside the neurosurgery department to discuss the reports of my CT scan that I'd had two weeks after my discharge. I entered the doctor's room; he smiled and asked me to take a seat. He was looking at some kind of X-ray. 'This is your brain. See the bones that are disjointed, the ones that are broken? We call it a skull fracture. It will take time to join but they will heal themselves. The brain is something that we can't plaster, it has its own process of healing. Continue with the rehab.'

'Yes!' I looked at it for a very long time, fighting back tears. Tears to celebrate the new life … or tears to forget the old life.

***

I was in the taxi, thinking about what the neurosurgeon just showed me – face to face with my birthmark, my scars and my broken bones. I remembered a day before leaving the hospital, an old woman took the vacant bed next to mine in my ward, after the girl who advised me about rehab had left. She kept on repeating to her visitors that she shared a room with a young girl who had been badly bashed by her boyfriend and didn't talk. I was startled by her preposterous imagination.

She was right in some ways; they were the scars of yesterday, which were left to be healed with this birth of today. She was right in seeing the ugliness of my old life but failed to see the profound birth. It did now have a mark – a birthmark.

Everyone has one; we mistake it for some kind of ugliness, seeking the help of plastic surgeons instead of rejoicing the beauty. I was happy with this beautiful scar, my birthmark.

The seeds of reincarnation, the embryo had been planted way back in Delhi; Melbourne just delivered me.

I looked at the final report of my discharge summary, it read:

Treatment and progress summary

36 y.o. F with fall of 40m down steep incline while bushwalking. Found by friends confused with head injury. Caused small ED secondary to skull fracture. GCS 13 AT SCENE (E3V4M6). Head strike and LOC.

Haemodynamically stable, equal power and sensation in limbs. Oriented to time and place. PEARL HR95-100. Saturating 100% on 4l NP.RR15-16. Tetanus shot given in emergency (5/11).

Injuries of the old life:

Small right-sided frontalemporal EDH 7mm, minimal midline shift.

left scalp laceration (3* sutures in ED on 5/11)

Small left-sided extra-axial haemorrhage

Right frontal lobe contusion

Traumatic SAH

Bilateral squamous temporal bone fractures

Bruising over left humerus (X-ray of left humerus unremarkable)

Bilateral knee lacerations

CT cervical/thoracic spine – no acute fracture management.

With my Baba

With my siblings

That's me, Maa in the background on Baba's 25 silver jubilee of Bancharamer Baagan

The Girls of the Missing Peace & I

The Girls of the Missing Peace

The face of Missing Peace

Guru's Machaan, Ashram Vrindhavan

Guru's Machaan, Ashram Vrindhavan

The river Yamuna flowing beside the Ashram, Vrindavan

Gates to Ashram

Friends for life

Christmas 2010

With Bethany

Aaron preparing for our climb

Morning of the Accident
5th Nov 2011,
Mt Cathedral, Australia

Image 1: Climbing deep into the forest
Image 2: Making the ascend
Image 3: Almost There
Mount Cathedral,
Australia

The flight for life. The helicopter taking me to The Alfred Hospital, Melbourne, Australia Air Ambulance Victoria rescued me

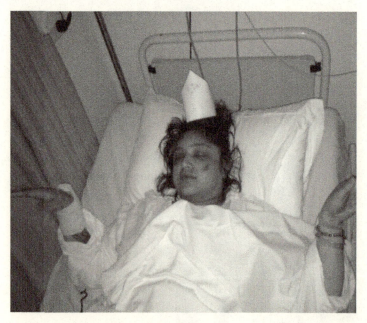

At the Alfred Hospital, Melbourne, Australia.

Melbourne City Skyline, Docklands, Australia

 # 23 DECEMBER 2011

> "True love has a habit of coming back."
>
> —Unknown

I was sitting in my lounge, resting myself on the couch with the support of a pillow, when I glanced across the room. The room was filled with cards from strangers from around the world and Australia. Harry's sisters spread the word of my accident to pray for my wellbeing – actually, to pray to God. It is expected from your family, but to be understood by complete strangers is not only humbling, but very touching. I knew prayers were also offered by Maa and Baba in the temples of Delhi, to Guru jee and Bala jee.

The first day when I entered the flat, it brought back the haunting memories of the night before I left for camp. I was frightened and it was a strange feeling, as if I was entering someone else's room. My nights were haunted with the fall and I could only see a strange woman falling from a cliff. I lost sleep as I slowly tried to introduce myself to the flat, to the rooms. I saw my prayer room, with photos of Maa and Baba and Guru jee, and then I knew who I was and what had happened.

I had nothing to do, so I thought the best way to pass time was to erase some old numbers to make place for the new. I sent texts to three numbers that had no names: 'Please kindly let me know who you are so I can clear my phonebook.' I got replies from two: one from a removalist and one from a courier who had delivered Harry's new bed the other day. I didn't get a reply from the third one until the next day. The message was, 'It is Franklin! The crappy Franklin who forgot to reply to all your messages.'

I was shocked. All along, he was hidden away like a priceless treasure. To unlock the mysteries of the universe, all I had to do was clear my phone. The final piece of the puzzle was always in front of me and I never looked at it. I thought I had erased him from my phone, but how could someone be erased so soon?

I filled him with information about my accident; I was hesitant as I didn't want his sympathy, but I shared anyway for the sake of the phoenix, his gift to me.

***

He was busy over Christmas, and it wasn't until the new year that we talked. I learned that on Christmas Day, he was with Sweets and they were in Sorrento to see the dolphins. I was with my sister's family to see the beach, feel the fresh air and to start the process of recovering. It was exhausting even to think about the travel, but then the exhaustion was dissolved in Franklin's words. We were headed in the same direction, but we still didn't cross paths or see each other. Maybe it wasn't the time.

By now my rehab was in full swing, with visits to the physio, occupational therapist and physiatrist to deliver me from my post-traumatic stress. Every day was a blessing and little things were an achievement for me. I had good days and sometimes I had bad days. I couldn't even sit down for a cup of coffee without getting slurred speech and trouble concentrating. I couldn't write anything, nor could I sleep. I had severe headaches and dizziness. But I took them as they came, a blessing to cherish what I had today. Not complaining but being grateful and thankful to everyone who was helping me and praying for my progress.

I was later diagnosed with impaired concentration and chronic fatigue. Cognitive issues were quite visible. At first, I forgot little things like names, but I gave it time and allowed myself to think. I maintained a diary and wrote down things to do. I stuck a blue tag on my fridge with the instructions given by the occupational therapist. My recovery was in progress and I made a truce with my head: 'You give me pain, but I will not complain as long as you don't defy me, such as by forgetting a name.'

Over the coming weeks, I invited Franklin to lunch. He was feeling low and thought he couldn't be of any use or good company. He was feeling low because his love 'Sweets' had gone back after her holidays in Melbourne with him. We had a good lunch; I cooked a meal which normally would take me a few hours, but took a good day. I was exhausted but I anticipated meeting him and it got me going.

***

'Ta-dahh!'

'What an entrance!' Franklin was shocked and happy with this sudden burst of emotion from me. We hugged and exclaimed how happy we were to see each other again. He was a bearded man now and looked very fragile, as if in mourning. I introduced him to Harry and Anthea. I made fish Bengali-style; fish is cooked for any auspicious occasion and today was an auspicious day.

We talked about our lives again. He rented his own place now and he and his ex had finally gone their separate ways. They only had their son in common now. He loved his son so much that he gave away the house to his ex so that she could bring up their son. He didn't fight for anything, not even money. He did all this out of love for his son.

We were talking on the balcony and everything he said was as if he was feeling guilty of what was happening around him. 'Please try forgiving yourself, Franklin. What you have with Sweets now is beautiful.'

He looked at my tattoo. 'It's beautiful. I'm getting mine done when I have some money and time … five grand, they quoted me. Bit by bit but I *will* get it done. One day.' Did he remember? He saw the cut on my head and his eyes were sad. I didn't want this day to be about me. It was a celebration of lost and found. 'Come on, let's have lunch.'

At the dining table, Harry was trying his best to lighten the mood and so was Helen. Franklin was very quiet but did not hold back on giving compliments for the good lunch to the chef. I was highly humbled. We were talking about places where I would like to travel – I was telling him my dream place was Paris. On the wall of my lounge that faced the dining table, I'd hung a big photo of the Eiffel Tower in black and white. He thought I'd gone to Paris, but no; I kept it on the wall to inspire myself to travel to Paris one day. He suggested I would love Spain. He was showing me photos of Paris when he visited Notre Dame and then we stumbled across a photo of Sweets. 'Oops! Sorry.'

'Don't be. It's okay.' I smiled.

After lunch, he was going through the books in my bookshelf and there was this book by Paulo Coelho, which was given to me by a friend. I didn't pay attention to the book, but I was watching him closely. 'It is a nice book,' I told Franklin.

Then Franklin took another book in his hand, which was recently gifted over Christmas by Brea, called *The Women of Letters*. 'There is a similar book for men too. I used to go into these book clubs, where we wrote letters and exchanged them with the men across the room. I wrote a letter to Sweets.'

'Wow!' I was happy for him.

I learned that Franklin and Sweets were very happy together and somewhere on the horizon, they would like to take it to the next level. I never knew he wasn't married to his ex, though he always knew that I was married. It was funny: we knew nothing of each other but somehow, we knew everything. 'So, what about you?'

'What about me? I'm happy the way I am. Today I have such beautiful friends – some new, some old and some lost ones.' He smiled at me.

We hugged each other goodbye and he touched the tattoo. I don't know why he did that. I silently hoped he remembered to stay in my life this time.

I walked back to my flat. It was the 8th of September when he found me in that little café. Today, after four months, this time I found him to lose him again. 'No, I will not cry,' I said to myself, 'I have to celebrate what I've found.'

I went into the apartment and sat at the dining table next to where Franklin had been sitting, facing the balcony. The skies were overcast – it would be raining soon. The skies understood my emotions, from the start of a sunny day to a rainy afternoon. Silently, those tears I fought back a few moments ago were inconsolable now – they just came out. Helen hugged me.

Harry and Helen were trying their best to make me laugh. The rain stopped and so did my tears. 'Come on! It's time for your afternoon walk.' They took me to the city. We laughed and I thanked God for His blessings to be surrounded by such good friends, and for sending Franklin back in my life.

It didn't matter if today we were just two good friends. He found love and that is crucial. That's the simple truth. I felt peace. What was most significant was that he saw the gift of the phoenix that helped me to see him again.

***

What is love? According to the dictionary, it is a profoundly tender, passionate affection or a deep attachment for another person.

To me it's not only feelings, but also devoting those feelings to one's conscious, which is the true essence of love. The sense to feel, to live through those feelings and to aspire to those sensibilities – that's what love is. Love never dies; it's always with us, among us, around us. We should not expect love to respond to us the same way we respond to other's affections. Because not everyone has the same feelings, everyone's love and interpretation of love is different.

But if we understand this, then there will never be any question of complications. The heart's door is fragile; at every knock it could collapse and the next day it would be on the mend again. It is up to us to take care of our feelings, the same way we safeguard our house.

Intensity of love doesn't guarantee veracity of love. Indeed, it is a very difficult process when it comes to love and devotion – the hardest part is analysing love. Most matters of love involve devotion until one can prove … but what is there to prove?

The simplest thing, naturally! Simply to prove how much love, devotion and trust one has in someone else's love. That also depends on how much love, devotion and trust one has in themselves. This is what we forget: the simplest equation to resolve love. When we cannot solve this, we play the blame game.

***

When I was in my mother's womb, I created a big fuss to enter the world. God was warning me, since then, that the world is too unrelenting for me. But against all odds, against that umbilical cord that fastened around my neck, I was delivered as a healthy eight-pound infant.

At the age of five, I fell from the terrace in our house in Kolkatta. It was the festival season, Goddess Durga's Puja ceremony. God was trying to tell me something then. But like every *puja*, Goddess Durga took everyone's prayers with her with the immersion of her idol in the Ganges; with her, she took the request she had from me too.

I was six years old when I was lost in the airport during a family summer holiday, but I was found because I had the will to look after myself. I always got by and I always found myself, no matter how lost I was.

It took a while for me to understand this – and life. But I've finally learnt to accept and live. Now it doesn't matter how my days are, good or bad. I've finally learned the truth. Now I know what happiness, sadness and peace are. They're like seasons; they come and go, never to last forever. I've learned now to leave without tears. I'm not alone, never was alone – just distracted seeing the truth of life.

Life is divided into two truths. Life can be a disappointment if we choose, and forever we will blame life to be a disappointment. The other truth is to rise above those disappointments.

It was as if life was trying to tell me, through the eyes of the girls of The Missing Peace and the people who crossed my path, where I've been until now. Life is indeed like a long journey and in that journey, I thought I was alone – but I had everyone with me, trying to tell me that I belong here, with myself, within myself.

There comes a time when bad takes a step back, to invite the good. Similarly, no one is bad; we characterise or brand people with good and bad. We invite people into our lives the same way we invite our feelings to dominate us. The way we feel sometimes leads to the people we meet across our journey of life.

The lotus flower also needs mud to grow and it's one of the most beautiful creations of God. I sometimes feel like that lotus flower. Though I've been given this beautiful gift of life, I chose to push myself into the mud and I would fight myself to grow beyond that which is false and ugly.

 # 9 SEPTEMBER 2016

> "Unable are the loved to die... For love is immortality."
>
> **Emily Dickenson**

Everywhere I looked, everything seemed to blossom and glow. I hated it. Inside I was nervous, hating myself, quietly withering – practically dying. I wanted to laugh at the whole world and tell you fools aloud not to be fooled by this glitter that the world is offering: 'It's all a fucking mirage.'

My legs were heavy, my thoughts were confused – cursing with every breath that I could hold, to condemn my brother and sister for not being here, leaving me with this thing to deal with. I didn't know what to do – how to react in such a situation. What was the appropriate thing to do, the appropriate language to speak and the appropriate thing to wear?

Just a few hours ago, Maa nudged me. I woke up crying in my own sleep. I didn't cry at the news when I received the text from Sumi, my sister: 'Baba is no more.' I just stood blank-faced, announcing to the entire meeting room, 'Oh! My dad just passed away; I have to go.' When I left the meeting room to gather my stuff, I remember people consoling me, but I don't know if I cried. I kept looking at the text message, the words eating my insides.

It had hardly been 24 hours since I'd landed and here I was, standing with Maa and a few relatives in the crematorium. It was the most surreal experience I ever had. I remember it was 5.00 am – dawn was lurking its way into the darkness, as if the skies were trying to tell me something. The only other companions we had were some stray dogs. 'What was that smell?' I questioned myself.

As soon as I entered the crematorium, I saw a pyre burning – the smell of flesh, how do I explain? It was a charred piece of meat with sandalwood and ghee poured on top, burning away. Was he a poor man or a rich man? My brain was spinning. I wanted to die when I walked slowly to Baba's side.

You see, we had to collect the ashes and travel 500 km to Haridwar. It's a Hindu tradition for the ashes to be scattered in the Ganges; one of the many Hindu traditions to attend *moksha*. Being a patriarchal society, it was always the son who had the right to light the pyre. If there's no son in the family, then the wife takes this right. I have a brother, or I should say I had a brother. He was not there to support in this crisis – just sitting in the airport like a coward on his wife's order, contemplating whether to come or not. Seriously, what was he questioning?

Such animosity now! I hated him even more. My gaze shifted to the clear sky. He wasn't coming.

Everybody was gathered at the pyre, the ashes in front of me. There was nothing, just grey warm sand – I would say still hot. It had been maybe a couple of hours since it last burned. 'Look for the spinal cord,' my aunty screamed. I wasn't ready for this. I closed my eyes. I thought if I opened my eyes it was just a bad dream, it would go away – I wanted my brain to shut down like it did a few weeks ago when I was walking the streets of Melbourne. I forgot who I was, where I was and what I was doing. I tried to cry then, but the tears wouldn't come.

I walked slowly towards the ashes. For a split second I thought I could do this, just like the fear of flying vanished with the news of Baba's death, but then there was this new fear and anxiousness. I wanted to cheat this day – nothing had happened, and Baba was just somewhere, hiding. He would be back soon.

No – he wasn't coming back.

I touched the hot ash; a sudden realisation silenced my thoughts. This was it: the last time I would hold him, touch him. How right was Maa when she always said that no one can speak about birth and death? It is only the soul that binds the body. I wanted to see that soul of my father – where did it go? I ran my fingers through the ashes – it felt so unreal. I came across his kneecaps, then the skeleton of his legs. I gulped my own vomit. By now, the smell from the pyre was overtaking my thoughts. I wanted to run away.

No one prepares anyone for death – and that's the whole reality. Why is it that when a child is born, everything is celebrated, but when death comes, everyone is sad? We pray for the dead to receive salvation and pray silently for the departed. Once again, I was at the crossroads of life – not so far away from the distant past.

On our way to Haridwar, Baba's ashes sat next to us in a brass pot carefully tied in a bag. I felt obligated not to hold him, as if he was saying he needed some space. I still ran my fingers over the bag.

When we reached, I saw my brother waiting at the gates. He called earlier to meet us there. I acted cool but deep inside I was angry and mourning at the same time.

When the priest took us to the back of the huge temple, I saw the river flowing that I had seen in my dreams so many times, but what I hadn't seen were bones and human remains.

The Ganges was floating in them and there were young boys diving in, searching for coins or even gold that was offered during the ceremony.

It was our turn to give away the ashes into the Ganges. One by one. When all was done I couldn't recognise which was Baba's among those thousand others that were floating.

I felt then I'd lost him forever; all I could hear was his words, 'Maybe I won't see you again,' the last visit. I felt like crying, but damn! The tears betrayed me again. I wanted to hit myself – as if that pain would bring me to tears.

After the dip at the Ganges to purify ourselves after performing the rites, I felt calm. The cold water of the Ganges flowing from the Himalayas made me feel better – as if it was a new beginning for me, the Ganges taking away all my pain. It was too much to feel.

'Have a good life,' is what I said to my brother when walking to the car for our return to Delhi. That was the last time I saw my brother.

After the thirteen days of rituals and priests coming to the house to read the Bhagavad Gita, Baba visited me in my dreams, blessing me and saying that there was a gift for me on the 13th of March. At that time, I didn't realise what it would be – but five months later I knew what it was. I began to write again, through a number of therapy sessions with my psychologist and help from all the therapy at the Royal Melbourne.

I cheated death twice. Once, falling from a mountain – and later, I almost took my life. When back from Delhi after Baba's funeral I had no money to pay rent and was on the verge of being kicked out of the house. I had two options: either face everything that was being offered, or silently go off to a deep sleep. I had taken three sleeping pills and a whole bottle of wine. My heart was racing faster, and I went numb, scared of what would happen. I wanted to stay awake, scared of death, but I had fallen into a deep sleep, only to be woken next day with the realisation I needed to call the psychologist for an appointment. I'm glad I did.

In the coming months, I would stand in line at the Salvation Army for food vouchers and sometimes a Coles card from my social workers. I went to the housing commission to find myself a room. But friends helped me. It was all too much for my family to comprehend my issues, as they were still dealing with Baba's loss – and in a few months, Jethu passed away too. The family was broken again. I forgot what it was to be hugged by my mother. I thought she needed me more; actually, it was I who needed her.

But in the coming months, life changed for me. I had a place to stay. Maa and my sister reunited. I would publish my book and travel to Paris, because life gave me another chance – Baba's blessings. When I look back to six years ago, that was the foundation laid before me, getting me closer to the truth. Change is transformative if we choose to embrace it and surrender to it. By taking our time to understand who we are and what we want to be, we'll never be far away from the truth.

I fought to comprehend what the neurologist told me about my disability, to fight mental health, and to come to terms with some truth about my physicality that I was in denial of for so long. I saw my new normal.

It was hard to lose my father. Everything happened in a span of a week. I look back at my life and it was not easy then, and I know sometimes in the future I will have challenges, but I've learnt and am brave enough to deal with it now.

It was a difficult situation to go back to the psychologist's chair. I was ashamed. I've always struggled with forgiveness. It's easy to say, but much more difficult to own it. I definitely made some bad choices, personally and financially, but no one forced me – they were my choices and I'm fully responsible. I still cannot own my peace with my brother; from my side I will hold the white flag. Maybe my story with him has a few more chapters. For now, it stays unwritten ... but definitely forgiven.

EPILOGUE

I remember a family friend of ours in India. I call her Anjali aunty. The day before I left for Melbourne, she told me that one day I would find myself in the service of others. I didn't know until now what she meant by that. The world is a mirror and we see our reflections in others.

It is a magical moment when we understand that the quest for love and peace is always around us, within us – and it is indeed a never-ending and never-dying process. Everyone tries to play their part sincerely, but we're accepted beyond judgments, with grace and kindness.

The accident was not only a medium for me to understand myself, but it also proved to be the medium for Harry. He saw where he belonged and with whom. He was dating Helen and Brea. Harry chose Helen over Brea because the accident gave him an insight of Helen's strength. It would be wrong to say that Brea doesn't possess those qualities but when the heart verifies the truth, there is no escape. Yes! There were tears and heartbreak and even condemnation for feeling cheated. Harry has healed me and so has Brea.

Brea and I are still friends today; she could have chosen not to be but we human beings are kind beyond our own suspicions, and sometimes we do rise above our own vindictive plight.

Helen and Harry had given me the gift of understanding that everything we do is important and taking risks is a valid part of the journey. If Helen didn't have her mobile with her on the mountain that day, I wouldn't have been saved today to write this, nor would I have become a writer if I wasn't pushed so hard to defy my accident. If it weren't for Franklin, I wouldn't have understood that there's always room for friendship, even beyond his love for Sweets. If it weren't for him, I wouldn't have read *By the River Piedra I Sat Down and Wept* by Paulo Coelho.

I look back and see that I have everything with me today. I have the love of twenty-four women of The Missing Peace, the dog's family to embrace the new with the old, my sister still here after all that we have been through, and Maa. I have kept Baba alive in my memories; not one day goes by that I don't miss him and because of his love, which has been unconditional in many ways, I can write this. I have the love of so many people that I'm at peace with myself. There is still a little room for a man's love; if it comes, I will endure it forever, and if it still doesn't come then there is no room for complaints, as love is within me always.

I have been healed by all these people healing me in their own special ways, silently bringing me closer to my truth. Their simplicity was (and is) as simple as my quest for my missing peace and love.

The accident happened on the 5th of November 2011, resulting in acquired brain injury. Seven years on, my life has changed forever. Tagore once described the Taj Mahal as '*a teardrop on the cheek of eternity*'. How can I not make this my statement?

Mt Cathedral is my entry to the life that I lead now. In 2016, five years after the accident, I had to accept a very hard truth about myself; it was hard not only to accept, but to comprehend my cognitive disability and mental health. Was this that last truth? There is a saying that sometimes, everything in life comes in threes, good or bad. I wasn't expecting that to land right on my lap. I had so much that I would hit rock bottom, but from there it was only going up. That's how I got through. It wasn't easy but it also wasn't difficult to dream about all the wonderful things. I used to say to myself, this shall soon pass – just like happy days. My journey is of this beautiful broken mind, the beautiful broken me who rose above her own shadows.

There is nothing in this world that cannot be saved by faith in oneself. Similarly, there is nothing so sabotaged that it cannot be saved with love. Because of this, I request everyone to believe in this certainty and in oneself. With this, we will somehow be led to life's truth – teaching us in our present to take control of the past and shape our future. I advocate knowing this through my own experiences, because without this certainty, we'd be forever incriminated for being obscure or fey.

ACKNOWLEDGEMENTS

I take this opportunity to thank the following people with my ample gratitude – whose stories, energy and wisdom have helped me to translate my own meaning of peace.

To my dearest Maa and Baba, for being my mother and father. Without your prayers and patience for me, I wouldn't be full of prayers, wisdom and patience today. Baba, thank you for sharing your stories and experiences with love, otherwise I wouldn't have understood your definition of love today. I miss you every day.

To Franklin, who forever will remain Franklin to the world and in some ways to me, I thank you for being here now – and for making an agreement with me to not disappear from my life again.

A big thank you Rosalie Ham for being the guide introducing the creative of world of Australia, even before I knew I had what it takes to be the crazy writer in me.

Thank you Nirmal and Arpita, for your abundant love and support.

To Les, Blaise and Kev for also shaping my writing career.

Thank you Beau for proof reading the initial draft and saying as it is, black and white.

My dearest brother from another mother Paul, who beautifully stood by me thick and thin and no matter what our brother sister relationship is, it blossoms better over a glass of gin, when I can drink with you telling me as it is.

To Naumi and Jahnu Barua, for always trusting my art and for those beautiful wisdom that you showered with during my stay in Mumbai. Mentoring by you both is a gift that I promise to take care of.

To my dearest Tonee jee and Manjit jee for your unconditional love and support; and Tonee jee for always encouraging me and my craft.

To Mitu and Roy thank you always for appreciating the writer in me.

To Avanti, who helped me to overcome shame: love has no age or boundaries. Your spirit drives me. Thank you for being in my life.

My dearest Babin, thank you for all the geeky conversations we have, especially of the cosmos; sparking an intellectual creative conversation and how we spoke about the Shiva *ling* theories such as being of ancient aliens.

To Kumud jee for always motivating and inspiring me to write.

A huge part of this book belongs to my three beautiful girlfriends Evie, Susan and Kim – fourteen years of craziness, *what a ride it has been*!

My beautiful sister united we stand and divided we fall, it's been tough few years but look at us now, how beautifully we are together with our dearest Maa.

Thank you to 'The Missing Peace' for bringing me closer to life. And to the unsung heroes of the Alfred Hospital, the paramedics and the Royal Talbot – the many nurses and doctors for giving me a new life. To the Royal Melbourne Allied Health in 2016–2017 for their understanding.

Acknowledgements

Last but not least, to Lalitha my agent who didn't give up when I did, always encouraging and motivating me with ideas about bring out the best in the manuscript. Also a big thank you to dearest Tanya for chopping the long sentences and editing what was rightly needed.

Experiences of my life and pieces of conversations with the new friends that I made along the way; they not only taught me but encouraged me to believe in love, hope and relationships again. They may not be unique, but to me they're priceless and they have created my history, making their way through the pages in this book. Their experiences about life have reflected into my present, my quest for life.

The story however is incomplete; and there are so many stories to explore for this accidental writer.

"Aaj Phir Jeene Ki Tamanna Hai." *I yearn to live again*!

ABOUT THE AUTHOR

Nandita Chakraborty was born in Kolkatta, India in a small conservative family which has always been associated with the arts. Her father won many accolades in Indian cinema; his film *In Search of Famine* was the first Indian film in a regional language to win the Silver Bear at the Berlin Film Festival in 1980.

Nandita's sense of creativity started at a young age. The whole house would be surrounded by action and glamour, where well-known artists would spark her creative mind at the dinner table or at her mother's dressing table.

Along with her siblings, she was sent out to boarding school at the age of seven in the hills of Meghalaya, India. A few years down the track the family settled in New Delhi, where she attended Sri Venketeswara University in New Delhi to study political science by day – and at night she would attend her fashion and visual merchandising school.

In her third year in college, she went on to pursue a Diploma in Visual Merchandising, leaving behind her career in political science. She began to work with a well-known designer in India, finding fame and fortune in that path – but it still didn't leave her creatively satisfied. Lying awake in her bedroom, she would often write poetry to herself. Secretly she wrote short stories about her adventures in her designing career. Often these would either land

About the Author

in the dustbin or make their way into the hands of junk dealers making paperbacks for grocery shopping.

In 2000 she came to Melbourne where she started her own fashion boutique, later going on to work in banking. It was not until 2008 she joined RMIT to do a short course in creative fiction writing under the mentoring of Rosalie. Ham Attending several book clubs, writing seminars and participating in many writing competitions, she met with some remarkable writers. Later she began to write short stories for the local newspaper and magazine in Melbourne.

She began writing in 2010. Her first book, mainly written for family and friends, was self-published in 2013. It's an autobiography called *Missing Peace: Love, Life & Me*, detailing her quest for peace, love and life.

In 2011, she met with an accident while rock climbing, falling 40 meters and acquiring traumatic brain injury. After several months in rehab, she continued working but in 2016 she was back in rehab. She has a disability which cannot be seen, also known as a blind disability, and suffers from vestibular migraine with permanent cognitive issues, resulting in fatigue. Nandita is also known as the accidental writer for her successful novellas *Meera Rising* and *Rosemary's Retribution*. The novellas were the product of her therapy rehab in 2016–2017.

Currently living in Melbourne, Australia, Nandita works as a library officer at Moreland city libraries. She is also a feature writer for Melbourne's leading Indian newspapers *The Indian Weekly* and *G'day India*. She's also a screen writer and has written few screenplays that are in developmental stages. In between her writings and therapies, she is constantly creating stories, new recipes and finding ways to keep her brain active.

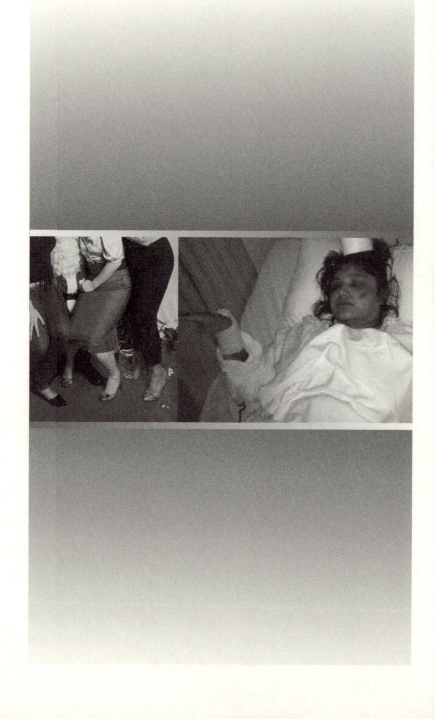

Made in the USA
Monee, IL
08 May 2022